By Celia's Arbour. A tale of Portsmouth Town. Reprinted from the "Graphic.".

Walter Besant, James Rice

By Celia's Arbour. A tale of Portsmouth Town. Reprinted from the "Graphic.".
Besant, Walter
British Library, Historical Print Editions
British Library
Rice, James
1878
3 vol. ; 8°.
12639.b.5.

The BiblioLife Network

This project was made possible in part by the BiblioLife Network (BLN), a project aimed at addressing some of the huge challenges facing book preservationists around the world. The BLN includes libraries, library networks, archives, subject matter experts, online communities and library service providers. We believe every book ever published should be available as a high-quality print reproduction; printed on- demand anywhere in the world. This insures the ongoing accessibility of the content and helps generate sustainable revenue for the libraries and organizations that work to preserve these important materials.

The following book is in the "public domain" and represents an authentic reproduction of the text as printed by the original publisher. While we have attempted to accurately maintain the integrity of the original work, there are sometimes problems with the original book or micro-film from which the books were digitized. This can result in minor errors in reproduction. Possible imperfections include missing and blurred pages, poor pictures, markings and other reproduction issues beyond our control. Because this work is culturally important, we have made it available as part of our commitment to protecting, preserving, and promoting the world's literature.

GUIDE TO FOLD-OUTS, MAPS and OVERSIZED IMAGES

In an online database, page images do not need to conform to the size restrictions found in a printed book. When converting these images back into a printed bound book, the page sizes are standardized in ways that maintain the detail of the original. For large images, such as fold-out maps, the original page image is split into two or more pages.

Guidelines used to determine the split of oversize pages:

• Some images are split vertically; large images require vertical and horizontal splits.
• For horizontal splits, the content is split left to right.
• For vertical splits, the content is split from top to bottom.
• For both vertical and horizontal splits, the image is processed from top left to bottom right.

12639,45.

BY CELIA'S ARBOUR.

A Tale of Portsmouth Town.

[REPRINTED FROM THE "GRAPHIC."]

BY

WALTER BESANT AND JAMES RICE,

AUTHORS OF

"READY-MONEY MORTIBOY," "THE GOLDEN BUTTERFLY," "MY
LITTLE GIRL," "WITH HARP AND CROWN," "THIS SON OF
VULCAN," "THE CASE OF MR. LUCRAFT," "WHEN THE
SHIP COMES HOME," "THE MONKS OF THELEMA,"
ETC., ETC.

IN THREE VOLUMES.
VOL. III.

LONDON:
SAMPSON LOW, MARSTON, SEARLE, & RIVINGTON,
CROWN BUILDINGS, 188, FLEET STREET, E.C.
1878.

CONTENTS OF VOL. III.

iv   *Contents.*

BY CELIA'S ARBOUR.

CHAPTER I.

LOVE'S VICTORY.

I SHALL premise that my story now becomes the journal of three days—every hour of which is graven on my memory. And I must tell the events which crowd that brief period as if I was actually present at all of them.

Our rejoicings and dinner-parties were all over
Outwardly, at least, we had all dropped back to
our old habits. I had no lessons to give, because
we were in holiday time, and divided my day
between Celia and Leonard, unless we were all
three together. But Celia was anxious; I was
waiting with a sinking at the heart for Wassielewski's signal; and every day the face of Mr.
Tyrrell grew more cloudy and overcast with care.
He was mayor for the year, as I think I have said
before, and had the municipal work in addition to
the business of his own office.

The first of these three days was June the 28th
—a week after Leonard's return. He had met
Celia every day—sometimes twice in the same day;
as yet he had said nothing.

"Suppose," he said, "Suppose, Laddy, that—I
only put a case, you know—that I were to meet
you and Celia in the Queen's Bastion; suppose
there should be no one else in the place——"

"Well?" I asked.

"Would it, I say, in such a contingency, occur to
you to have an appointment elsewhere?"

I forget whether Perseus had fallen in love with
Andromeda before the slaying of the dragon; if

so, the agitation in the breast of the warrior must have been greatly intensified, especially when he found he had only just arrived in time.

I told him that it was a clear breach of trust; that Celia was allowed to come out with me in a tacit understanding that there should be no love-making; that I was a male duenna: that I should be ever after haunted by the knowledge of the crime; that I should be afraid to face her father; that Herr Räumer — but, after all, it mattered nothing what Herr Räumer thought; and—finally, I acceded, promised to efface myself, and wished him success.

I do not know how it was that on the morning of that 28th day of June, Celia looked happier and brighter than she had done for weeks. She was dressed, I remember, in some light silver-grey muslin dress, which became her tall and graceful figure, and the sweet calm face above it. I knew every shade of her face; I had seen it change from childhood to womanhood; I had watched the clouds grow upon it during the trouble of the last few weeks; I had seen the sunshine come back to it when Leonard came home again, to bring us new hope. The dreariness was gone out of her eyes, with the strange sad look of fixed speculation and the dreamy gloom.

"Yes, Laddy," she said, catching my look and understanding it. "Yes, Laddy, I am more hopeful now. Leonard has come home again. I do not know how, but I am certain that he will help us."

On this morning there was a Function of some kind—a Launch—a Reception—a Royal Visit—going on in the Dockyard. From Celia's Arbour we could see the ships gay with bunting; there were occasional bursts of music; it must have been a Launch, because the garrison bands were playing while the people assembled in the shed, the naval and military officers in full uniform; the civil servants in the uniform of the Dockyard Volunteers —not those of 1860, but an earlier regiment, not so efficient, and with a much more gorgeous uniform; ladies in full war-paint, each in her own uniform, prepared to distract the male eye from contemplation too prolonged of naval architecture; the Mayor and Aldermen in gown and gold chain, splendid to look upon, in official seats, ready with an address; and no doubt, though one could only see him, as well as the Corporation, with the eyes of imagination, there would be among them all Ferdinand

Brambler, note-book in hand, jerking his head up
at the sky and making a note; looking at his watch
and making a note; gazing for a few moments
thoughtfully at the crowd and making a note—all
in the Grand Historical Style—and not at all as if
he was calculating the while what items of domestic
consumption this Ceremony would "run to."

Presently, turning from the contemplation of the
flags and discussion of hidden splendours we saw,
mounting the grass slope, with the most hypocritical
face in the world, as if his coming was by the merest
accident, Leonard himself.

"You here, Leonard?"

"Yes, Celia." Now that I looked again, I saw
that his face had a grave and thoughtful expression.
It was that of a man, I thought, who has a thing to
say. She read that look in his eye, I believe,
because she grew confused, and held me more
tightly by the arm.

It did not seem to me that there was any occasion
here for beating about the bush, and pretending to
have appointments. Why should I make up a story
about leaving something behind? So I put the
case openly. "Leonard has asked me to leave you
with him, Cis, for half an hour. I shall walk as far

as the Hospital and sit down. In half an hour I
will come back."

She made no reply, and I left them there—alone.
There was no one but themselves in the Queen's
Bastion, and I thought, as I walked away, that if
Heaven had thought fit to make me a lover like
the rest of mankind, there was no place in the world
where I would sooner declare my love than Celia's
Arbour—provided I could whisper the tale into
Celia's own ear.

Half an hour to wait. At the end of the long
straight curtain, in the middle of which was the
Lion's Gate, with its little octagonal stone watch-
tower, and where the wooden railings fenced off
the exercise-ground of the Convalescent Hospital, I
found the little Brambler children playing, and
stood watching them. That took up fully ten
minutes. Three tall, gaunt soldiers, thin and pale
from recent sickness, were on the other side of the
fence watching them too. One of them bore on
his cap the number of Leonard's regiment.

I asked him if he knew Captain Copleston.

He laughed. "Gentleman Jack?" he asked.
"Why, who doesn't know Gentleman Jack? I
was in the ranks with him. Always a gentleman,

though, and the smartest man in the regiment. It was him as took the Rifle Pit. That was the making of him. And no one grudged him the luck. Some sense, making *him* an officer."

From which I gathered that there were other officers in the regiment who had not commended themselves to this good fellow's admiration.

The Bramblers, headed by Forty-six, now a sturdy lad of twelve, were celebrating an imaginary banquet, in imitation of last night's tremendous and unexpected feed. The eldest boy occupied the chair, and ably sustained the outward forms of carving, inviting to titbits, a little more of the gravy, the addition of a piece of fat, a slice of the silver side, another helping, pressing at the same time a cordial invitation on all to drink, with a choice of liquors which did infinite credit to his information and his inventive faculty, and sending about invisible plates and imaginary goblets with an alacrity and hospitality worthy of a One-eyed Calender at the feast of a Barmecide or a super at a theatrical banquet. It was an idyllic scene, and one enjoyed it all the more because the children— their breakings-out were better already—entered into the spirit of the thing with such keen delight,

because one knew that at home there was awaiting
them the goodly remnant of that noble round of
beef; and because the historio-graphically gifted
Ferdinand had found fresh and worthy subjects for
his pen, which might result, if judiciously handled,
in many legs of mutton.

By a combination of circumstances needless here
to explain, Forty-six subsequently became, and is
still, a shorthand reporter. He does not go into
the Gallery of the House, because he prefers re-
porting public dinners, breakfasts, and all those
Functions where eating and drinking come into
play. You may recognise his hand, if you remember to think of it, when you read the reports
of such meetings in the accuracy, the fulness, and
the feeling which are shown in his notice of the
viands and the drinks. It is unnecessary to say
that he has never parted with the twist which
characterised him as a boy, and was due to the
year of his birth, and he may be seen at that
Paradise of Reporters, the Cheshire Cheese, taking
two steaks to his neighbour's one; after the steaks,
ordering a couple of kidneys on toast, being twice
as much as anybody else, and taking cheese on a

like liberal scale. He is said, also, to have views of great breadth in the matter of stout, and to be always thirsty on the exhibition of Scotch whisky.

When I was tired of watching the boys and girls, I strolled part of the way back, and sat down on the grassy bank in the shade, while the thoughts flew across my brain like the swallows flitting backwards and forwards before me, in the shade of the trees and in the sunshine.

Leonard and Celia on the Queen's Bastion together. I, apart and alone. Of two, one is taken and the other left. They would go away together, hand in hand, along a flowery lane, and I should be left to make my lonely pilgrimage without them. Who could face this thing without some sadness? All around were the sights and sounds which would weave themselves for ever in my brain with recollections of Celia and of Leonard and the brave days of old. How many times had she and I leaned over the breastwork watching the little buglers on the grassy ravelin beyond the moat practising the calls, all a summer afternoon? How many times had we laughed to see the little drummer boys marching backwards and forwards,

each with his drum and pair of sticks, beating the
tattoo for practice with unceasing rub-adub?
Down in the meadows at my feet, where the
buttercups stood tall and splendid, we had wandered
knee-deep among the flowers, when Celia was a
tiny little girl. The great and splendid harbour
behind me, across which we loved to sail, in and
out among the brave old ships lying motionless
and dismasted on the smooth surface, like the aged
one-legged tars sitting on their bench in the sunshine, quiet and silent, would for ever bear in its
glassy surface a reflection of Celia's sweet face.
Listen: there is the booming of guns from the
Blockhouse Fort; a great ship has come home from
a long cruise. Is every salute in future to remind me
of Celia? Or again—do you hear it? The muffled
drum; the fife; the dull echo of the big drum at
intervals. It is the Dead March, and they are
burying a soldier, perhaps one of the men from
India, in the churchyard below the walls. Backwards with a rush goes the memory to that day
when Leonard stood with me watching such a
sight, and refusing to believe that such a man, poor
private that he was, had failed. No doubt 'twas a

brave and honest soldier—there is the roll of
musketry over his grave—God rest his soul!
Down below, creeping sluggishly along, go the
gangs of convicts armed with pick and spade. No
funeral march for them when their course is run;
only the chaplain to read the appointed service;
only an ignoble and forgotten grave in the mud of
Rat Island; and perhaps in some far-off place a
broken-hearted woman to thank God that her
unfortunate, weak-willed son has been taken from
a world whose temptations were too much for his
strength of brain. Why, even the convicts will
make me think of Celia, with whom I have so many
times watched them come and go.

All the life of the garrison and seaport town is
in these things. The great man-o'-war coming
home after her three years' cruise; the launch in
the Dockyard; the boys practising the drum and the
bugle; the burial of the private soldier; the gang of
prisoners—everything is there except Wassielewski
and the Poles.

All our petty provincial life. Only that? Why,
there is in it all the comedy of humanity, its
splendour, its pride, its hopes, its misery, its death.

I could look at none of these things—nor can I now—without associating them with the days and the companions of my youth.

Sad were the thoughts of those few minutes—a veritable *mauvais quart d'heure*—for I saw that I should speedily lose her who was the sunshine of my life. I did not think of the many visits we should pay each other, the happy greetings, after days of separation, in the future. I thought only of the barren hours dragging themselves wearily along, without Celia. The rose of love that had sprung up unbidden in my heart was plucked indeed, but the prickings of its thorns in my soul made me feel that the plant was still alive. Was, then, Celia anything more to me than a sister? I never had a sister, and cannot tell. But she was all the world to me, my light, my life—although I knew that she would never marry me. What, I said to myself, for the half-hour was almost up,— what can it matter so long as Celia finds happiness, if I do not? What selfishness is this that would repine because her road lies along the lilies while mine seems all among the thorns? After all, to him who goes cheerfully among the appointed thorns, a thousand pretty blossoms spring up presently beneath his foot. And among the briars, to lighten the labours of the march, there climbs and twines the honeysuckle.

While I was sitting with these thoughts in my brain, this is what was going on at the Queen's Bastion.

Leonard and Celia face to face, the faces of both downcast, the one because she was a girl, and knew beforehand what would be said; the other because he reverenced and feared the girl before him, and because this was the fatal moment on which hung the fulfilment of his life. Above them the great leafy branches of the giant elm, prodigal in shade.

Leonard broke the silence.

"I have been looking for this hour," he began, stammering and uncertain, "for five long years. I began to hope for it when I first left the town. The hope was well-nigh dead, as a child's cry for the moon ceases when he finds it is too far off, while I fought my way up from the ranks. But it awoke again the day I received the colours, and it has been a living hope ever since, until, as time

went on, I began to think that some day I might
have the opportunity of telling you—what I am
trying to tell you now.   The time has come, Celia,
and I do not know how to frame the words."

She did not reply, but she trembled.   She
trembled the more when he took her hand, and
held it in his own.

" My dear," he whispered, " my dear, I have no
fitting words.   I want to tell you that I love you.
Answer me, Celia."

" What am I to say, Leonard ?"

" Tell me what is in your heart.   Oh, my darling,
tell me if you can love me a little in return ?"

" Leonard—Leonard !"   She said no more.   And
he caught her to his heart, and kissed her, in that
open spot, in broad daylight, on the forehead,
cheeks, and lips, till she drew herself away, shame-
faced, frightened.

" My dear," it was nearly all he could say—and
they sat down presently, side by side upon the
grass, and he held both her hands together in his.
"My dear, my love, what has become of all the
fine speeches I would have made about my humble
origin, and devotion ?   They all went out of my

head directly I felt the touch of your hand. I
could think of nothing, but—I love you—I love
you. I have always loved you since you were a
little child ; and now that you are so beautiful—so
sweet, so good—my queen of womanhood—I love
you ten times as much as I ever thought I could,
even when I lay awake at night in the trenches,
trying to picture such a moment as this. My love,
you [are too high for me. I am not worthy of
you."

"Not worthy ? Oh! Leonard—do not say that.
You have made me proud and happy. What can
you find in me, or think that there is in me, that you
could love me so—for five long years ? Are you
sure that you are not setting up an ideal that you
will tire of, and be disappointed when you find the
reality ?"

Disappointed ? He—and with Celia ?

He released her hands, and laid his arm around
her waist.

"What a mistake to make ! To be in love with
a woman and to find her an angel. My dear, I am
a man of very small imagination—not like Laddy,
who peoples his Heaven with angels like yourself,

and lives there in fancy always—and I am only
certain of what I see for myself. What I see is
that you are a pearl beyond all price, and that I
love you—and, Celia, I am humble before you.
You shall teach me, and lead me upwards to your
own level, if you can."

When I came back, the half-hour expired, they
were sitting side by side on that slope of tall grass
still. But they were changed, transformed. Celia's
face was glowing with a new light of happiness; it
was like the water in the harbour that we had once
seen touched by the light of the rising sun; her
cheeks were flushed, her eyes were glistening with
tears; one hand lay in Leonard's, and round her
waist was Leonard's arm.

As for her lover, he was triumphant; it was
nothing to him that he was making demonstrative
love in this public place, actually a bastion on the
ramparts of Her Majesty's most important naval
station and dockyard. To be sure there was no
one to see them but the swallows, and these birds,
whose pairing time was over for the season, had
too much to do fly-catching—the serious business
of life being well set in for swallows in the month

of June—to pay much regard to a pair of foolish mortals.

"Come, Laddy," he cried, springing to his feet and seizing her by the hand, while Celia rose all as blushing as Venus Anadyomene, "be the first to wish that Celia may be happy. She has been so foolish, this dear Celia of ours, this dainty little Cis that we love so much, as to say that she will take me just as I am, for better and for worse." He took her hand again with that proud and happy look of triumphant love, as if he could not bear to let her go for a moment, and she nestled close to him as if it was her place, and she loved to be near him. "There is a foolish maiden for you. There is an indiscreet and imprudent angel who comes down from the heavens to live with us on earth. Congratulate her, Laddy, my dear old dreamer. I am so happy."

Celia shyly drew her hand away, and came over to me as if for protection. I saw how her proud and queenly manner was in some way humbled, and that she was subdued, as if she had found her master.

She laid her hand upon my shoulder, in her

caressing way, which showed me that she was happy, and then I began to congratulate them both. After that I made them sit down on the grass, while I sat on the wheel of the gun-carriage, and I talked sense and reason to them. I told them that this kind of engagement was one greatly to be deprecated, that it was highly irregular not to go first to head-quarters, and to ask permission of parents. That to confess to each other, in this impetuous way, of love, and to make promises of marriage, were things which even Mr. Pontifex, when the passions of his youth were so strong as to make him curse the Goose, had not to repent of; that Mrs. Pontifex had always recommended Celia to follow her own example, and wait till she was of ripe and mature years before marrying any one, and then to marry a man some years younger than herself; that they ought to consider how a soldier's life was a wandering one, and a Captain's pay not more than enough for the simple necessaries; that they might have to wait till Leonard was a Field-Marshal before consent could be obtained; that the Captain would be greatly astonished; that neither he nor I intended to allow Leonard to carry Cis away with him for a long time to come, nor had we dreamed that such a thing would follow when we welcomed him home. Many more things I added in the same strain, while Leonard laughed, and Cis listened, half-laughing and half-crying, and then, because the occasion was really a solemn one, I spoke a little of my mind. They were good, and bore with me as I leaned over the old gun and talked, looking through the embrasure across the harbour.

I reminded Leonard how, five years ago, he had left us, with the resolution to advance himself, and the hope of returning and of finding Celia free. Never any man, I told him, had such great good fortune as had fallen on him, in getting all he hoped and prayed for. And then I tried to tell him how for five years the girl whose hand he had won had been growing in grace as well as beauty, feeding her mind with holy thoughts, and living in forgetfulness of herself; how it had been an education to me to be with her, to watch her, to learn from her, and to love and cherish her—and then Celia sprang up and interrupted me, and fell upon my neck, crying, and kissing me. Oh! happy day!

oh! day of tears and sunshine! Oh! day fruitful
of blessed memories, when for once we could bare
our hearts to each other, and show what lay there
hidden. No need any more to pretend. I loved
her, and I always had loved her. She loved me
too, if not in the same way, what matter?

"Well, it was all over, Celia was promised to
Leonard.   And yet it seemed as if it was only all
begun.   Because, after a little while, Cis turned to
me with a cry, as one who remembers something
forgotten.

"Laddy, what about Herr Räumer?"

She and I looked at each other in dismay.
Leonard laughed.

"There is Perseus," I said, pointing to him.
"He is strong and brave. He is come to rescue
Andromeda.   What did I tell you, Cis, the day
before he kept his promise?"

She had not forgotten one word about the
loathly monster and the distressful maiden.

"Now it has all come true," I said. "Meantime,
the first thing is to tell the Captain. And that I
shall go and do this minute. You two will come on
when you please—when you are tired of each other."

Leaving them behind me hand in hand was like plunging at once into the loneliness which loomed before me when they two should be gone. One had no right to be sad. I had enjoyed the companionship of Celia for five years, all to myself; it could not be expected that I was to have her exclusive society for all my life. Besides, there was Poland—it really was hard to keep one's thoughts in that dark groove of revenge; I constantly forgot my wrongs and my responsibilities. Nor did I even, I fear, thoroughly realise the delights of battle, and the field of patriotic glory.

At the bottom of the slope then came to meet me the very man—old Wassielewski himself. He was radiant.

Without a word of preface, he cried out as he seized me by the hand :

"You are in luck. To-morrow they will call upon you."

"Who ?"

"The deputies from Basle, Geneva, London, and Paris. They will call upon you at three, with me. Be at home to meet them."

"And when—Wassielewski ?"

"When do we begin? At once; next week we must start. Courage, boy; you go to avenge the blood of your father. To-morrow—to-morrow—at three."

He waved his arms like the sails of a windmill.

Just then the bands in the yard, amid a deafening shout, because the ship was launched, struck up a splendid march.

"Listen," he cried. "That is an omen. Hear the music which welcomes the news of another Polish rebellion. A good omen. A good omen."

He sped swiftly away.

But it was a wedding march, and I thought of Leonard and Celia.

CHAPTER II.

THE KEY OF THE SAFE.

I WAS walking along the street after leaving this pair of lovers, full of thought, with my eyes on the ground, when I was aware of a voice calling my name. It was Augustus Brambler tearing along the pavement without a hat, a quill—Augustus would never descend to the meanness of a steel pen while in the Legal—still behind one ear, his coat-tails flying behind him, enthusiastically anxious to execute an order from the Chief. It was a simple message, asking me to step in and see Mr. Tyrrell. I complied, and turned back.

"And the children?" I asked.

"Better," Mr. Pulaski. "The Breakings-out have almost disappeared, thanks to an increase of Affluence. My brother Ferdinand is hard at work on his new series of papers. He calls them 'Reminiscences of the Crimea,' compiled from Captain Copleston's private information combined with the back numbers of the *Illustrated London News*, and the morning's Launch will be new boots all round. I don't think," he added in a whisper, "that the Chief is very well. Herr Räumer was with him this morning before he went into the Yard, and when he sent for me just now he was pale, and shivered. No one knows what we lawyers go through : no one can guess the wear and tear of brain. Dear me ! On Saturday night I often tell Mrs. Brambler that I feel as if another day would finish me off. But then Sunday comes, when Ferdinand and I can sit over our wine like gentlemen, and rest. Here we are, Mr. Pulaski," sinking his voice to a whisper. "I must return to a most important Case. Talk of intricacy ! Ah !"

Mr. Tyrrell was leaning against the mantel-shelf, looking, as Augustus said, anything but well. The Mayor's robes lay in his arm-chair, and round his neck still hung the great gold chain of office. Usually a high-coloured, florid man, with a confident carriage, he was now pale and trembling. His hands trembled; his lips trembled; his shoulders stooped. What was it that had placed him in another man's power?"

"Ladislas," he groaned, "I wish I were dead!"

That seems, certainly, the simplest solution of difficulties. I suppose every man, at some crisis in his fortune, has wished the same. At such times, when it seems as though everything was slipping under one's feet, and the solid foundation of wealth, honour, name, all the fabric of years, was tumbling to pieces like a pack of cards, even the uncertainty of the dread Future seems easier to face than the changes of the Present. Here was a man who mounted steadily, swiftly, without a single check, up the ladder of Fortune. He had saved money, bought houses, owned lands, possessed the best practice in the town, held municipal distinctions, was the envy of younger men and the admiration of his own contemporaries; and now, from some real or fancied power which this German possessed over him, he was stricken with a mortal terror and sickness of brain.

"I wish I were dead!" he repeated.

" Tell me what has happened, Mr. Tyrrell."

" He has been here again. That is nothing—he always is here. But he came with a special purpose last night. He came to say that he wanted an answer."

" Wants an answer ?"

" Celia must give him her decision."

" I am very—very glad, Mr. Tyrrell," I said, " that he did not want it yesterday morning. I will tell you why presently."

" He is jealous of young Copleston. Says Celia sat up all night with him and you when he came home. Is that true ?"

" Quite. We had so much to say that we did not separate till five in the morning."

" To be sure, you were all then children together. Why, you used to play in the garden and on the walls——"

" And so Herr Räumer is jealous ?" I asked, interrupting.

" He is mad with jealousy. He accuses me of fostering an attachment—as if I know anything about attachments !—he declares that he must have an answer to-morrow morning, and if it is not favourable——"

"My dear friend and benefactor," I said, "suppose it is not favourable. Can he take away your daughter? Can he rob you of your money? What can he do to you?"

"I dare not tell—even you, Laddy," he replied. "Money? No. He cannot touch my possessions. My daughter? No; he cannot carry her off. But he can almost do as bad. He can—he can—lower me in the eyes of the world; he can proclaim—if he will—a thing that men who do not know the whole truth will judge harshly. And he will disgrace me in the eyes of my daughter."

I was silent, thinking what to say.

Presently I ventured to ask him whether it would not disgrace him more in the eyes of Celia for him to lend his favour to a suit so preposterous.

He groaned in reply.

"You do not know, Laddy," he said, "the trouble I have had to build up a name in this place, where I began as a boy who swept the office, the son of a common labourer. My brothers are labourers still, and content with their position. My sisters are labourers' wives, and content as well. I am the great man of the family. I had much to contend

with, want of education, poverty, everything but
ability. I am sure I had that because I sur-
mounted all, and became—what I am. Then I
married into a good family, and took their level.
And the old low levels were forgotten. Why, if all
the world were to remind each other aloud that I
once swept out an office, it would not matter."

"Of course not, sir. Pray go on."

"It is fifteen years ago, when Herr Räumer
first came to the town. He had a plausible
tongue and wheedled himself into the confidence
of all whom he cared to know. He wanted to know
me. He made me his lawyer—sent round that
great safe, where it has been ever since, and used
to sit with me in the evening talking affairs. There
was nothing in the town too small for him to inquire into; he wanted the secret history of everything: and he got it from me; I violated no confidence of clients, but told him all I knew,"

"Did he talk much about the Poles?"

"He was, at first, very inquisitive about the
Poles. Said he sympathised with them—I did not,
so I had little to tell him. Then came the time
when they made the railway on our side of the
harbour——"

He paused for a moment.

" ——that was the fatal time. I yielded to his instigations, and, together, we——never mind what it was, Laddy. It was nothing that could bring me within the power of the Law, but it was an action which, stated in a certain way, would ruin me for ever in the town."

Successful men, I think, are apt to over-estimate the opinion which men have formed of them. They know that they are envied for their success, which is real; and they easily persuade themselves that they are admired for their virtues, which are imaginary. I do not believe that the town at large would have cared twopence if Herr Räumer had gone on to the balcony of the old Town Hall, and after sticking up a glove in the old fashion of the burgesses when a Town Function was about to begin, such as the opening of the fair, had there in clear and ringing tones denounced the great Mr. Tyrrell of such and such a meanness. They would have lifted their eyebrows, talked to each other for a day, reflected in the morning that he was rich and powerful, and then would have gone on as if nothing had happened. Because I do not think that any man in the place, however un-successful, believed in his heart that Mr. Tyrrell was a bit more virtuous than himself. But that the lawyer would not understand.

I think that one of Rochefoucald's maxims is omitted in all the editions. It has somehow slipped out. And it is this :

" Every man believes himself more virtuous than any other man. If the other man is found out, that proves the fact."

I was thinking out this moral problem, and be-ginning to test its truth by personal application to my own case, when I was roused by the conscious-ness that Mr. Tyrrell was talking still.

" ——Terrible and long labour in building a name as a Christian as well as a lawyer——good opinion of the clergy——"

It was very wonderful, but the theory did seem to fit marvellously well. I really did believe my-self quite as good as any of my neighbours—except Celia and the Captain—and better than most : much better than the Reverend John Pontifex.

" Tell me what you think, Laddy."

" I think, sir," I replied, " that I would lay the case

before the Captain, and ask his opinion. I know what it will be."

" You think——"

" I know that he will say, ' Laugh at him, and tell him to do the worst. Let him tell a miserable old story to all the town, but let Celia follow her own heart.' And another thing, Mr. Tyrrell—Celia's heart is no longer free."

" What ? Was he right ?"

" Quite right. Herr Räumer is a very clever man, and he seldom makes a mistake. Half an hour ago Celia listened to Leonard Copleston, and they are now engaged."

" It only wanted that," he replied with a groan.

This looked as if things were going to be made cheerful for the lovers.

" Will you see the Captain if he comes to you ? Or, better still, will you go yourself and talk things over with him ? It is half-past twelve, and he will be home by this time. And tell him all."

" I *must* have advice," he murmured. " I feel like a sinking ship. The Captain will stand by me whatever happens. Yes, Laddy—yes. I will go at once—at once——"

He rose, and with trembling hands began to search for his hat.

It was standing on the safe—the closed safe with the name of " Herr Räumer " upon it in fat white letters.

Mr. Tyrrell shook his fist at the door.

"You are always here," he cried, "with your silent menace. If you were open for five minutes, —if I had the key in my hands for only half a minute—I should know what answer to give your master."

He left me, and went out into the street, I after him. But he forgot my presence, and went on without me, murmuring as he went in the misery and agitation of his heart.

I suppose it was the pondering over this successful man as over a curious moral problem, and a certain uplifting of heart as I reflected that there was nothing at all for me to be ashamed of, even if I was found out, that laid me more than commonly open to temptation.

At all events it was then that I committed the meanest action in my life—a thing which whenever I meet my accomplice, even after all these years, makes me blush for shame.

My innocent accomplice was no other than little Forty-four.

As I was passing the Bramblers' house in Castle Street, Mr. Tyrrell being some twenty yards ahead of me, and going straight away to consult with the Captain, I not being wanted at all, I thought I would call upon my friends. No one was at home except Forty-four, who was sitting before the open kitchen window sewing and crooning some simple ditty to herself. Her mother was gone a-marketing—that was good news. Uncle Ferdinand, who had received an advance upon his series of papers called " Personal Recollections of the War " —everybody remembers what a sensation those articles caused—was gone out with his note-book to attend the Launch. Augustus Brambler was at his post, no doubt engaged on his labyrinthian case. The children were all on the walls where I had left them playing their little game of Feasting. And Forty-four was in charge of the family pot, which was cheerfully boiling on the fire.

She looked up with her bright laugh.

" Come into the kitchen, Mr. Pulaski, if you don't mind. I've something to tell you."

" What is it ?" I asked. " Are things looking better ?"

" Oh ! yes. Thanks to you know who. We had a dreadful time, though. The man the people call Tenderart—do you know him ?"

I knew him and his satellite of old.

" He is our landlord, and he came to take the things to make up the rent. There he stood and began to pick out the things to put in a cart. Uncle Ferdinand asked for time, and the man only laughed. Then Uncle Ferdinand banged his head against the wall and said this was the final Crusher, and we all cried. Then papa ran to get an advance from Mr. Tyrrell."

" Did you ask Herr Räumer ?"

" Yes ; I went up to ask him—and he said, politely, that he never helped anybody on prin- ciple. Well, papa got the advance, but it was stopped out of his salary, and so—you see—we have had very little to eat ever since. But Ten- derart was paid, and he went away."

" I see ; and now things are better ?"

" Yes. Because Uncle Ferdinand has found something to write about. And papa has got the most beautiful idea for making all our fortunes. See."

She opened a paper which lay upon the table, and showed it to me. It was written in a clerkly hand, partly couched in legal English, and referred to a scholastic project. So that in this document the threefold genius of Augustus was manifest.

"ROYAL COLLEGIATE ESTABLISHMENT
"*for the Education of both Sexes*,
"Conducted by the BROTHERS BRAMBLER.

"The object of this Institution is to impart to the young an education to fit them for the Learned Professions, for Commerce, for the Legal, the Scholastic, or the Clerical. Pupils will be received from the age of eight to fifteen. The College will be divided into two divisions, that for the ladies under the management of Mrs. Brambler, a lady highly connected with the Royal Naval Service, and Miss Lucretia Brambler."

"That's me," said Forty-four, ungrammatically.

"I thought you had no name," I said.

"Mr. Ferdinand Brambler, the well-known Author, will undertake the courses of History,

Geography, Political Economy, and English Composition. Mr. Augustus Brambler will superintend the classes of Latin, Euclid, Arithmetic, and Caligraphy——"

"My dear, when is the college to be started?"

"Oh! not yet," cried Forty-four. "When we are a little older, and all able to take a part in the Curriculum. Fancy the greatness!"

"Yes. It is almost too much, is it not? Don't set your heart too much on things, Forty-four." I did not finish the document, and returned it. The poorer Augustus grew, the more brilliant were his schemes. So Hogarth's starving poet sits beneath a plan of the mines of Potosi. "Is Herr Räumer at home?"

" I think he is gone out. Shall I run up to see?"

We went up together. I had nothing to say, and no reason for calling, but I was excited and restless.

He was not in his rooms. The table was littered and strewn with foreign papers, German, French, and Russian. The piano was littered with his songs—those little sentimentalities of student life of which he was never tired. There was the usual strong smell of recent tobacco in the place, and—it caught my eye as I was going away—there lay in an inkstand on the table—a temptation.

It was the Key of the Safe.

I turned twice to go, twice I came back, drawn by the irresistible force of that temptation. It riveted my eyes, it made my knees tremble beneath me, it seemed to drag my hand from my side, to force the fingers to close over it, to convey itself, by some secret life of its own, to my pocket, and once there, to urge me on to further action.

"Mr. Pulaski," cried Forty-four, "why are you so red in the face? What is the matter?"

"Hush," I whispered, "stay here for five minutes, Forty-five—if Herr Räumer comes home, bustle about and prevent his touching the table. And say nothing—promise to say nothing."

She promised, understanding no word.

I furtively descended the stairs, I crept swiftly, in the shade of the wall, though it was of course broad daylight, looking backwards and forwards, though there were only the usual people in the street, with beating heart and flushed face, towards Mr. Tyrrell's office. The outer door was open, that was usual; I pushed into the hall, and silently turned the handle of the chief's own office. It was not locked—they did not know he was out—there was, of course, no one in the room. Like some burglar in the dead of night I crept noiselessly over the carpet to open the safe.

It was done.

I was back in the street, the key in my hand; I was back at the Bramblers' house, I was upstairs again, the key was restored to its place. I seized Forty-four by the hand, and hurried her downstairs.

"What is it?" she asked again.

"Remember, Forty-four, you have promised to tell no one. It was the key of Herr Räumer's safe. I borrowed it for five minutes—for Celia Tyrrell's sake."

She promised again—nothing, she said, would make her tell any one. No one should know that I had been in the room : she entered as zealously into the conspiracy as if she was a grown woman married to a St. Petersburg diplomatist, and engaged in throwing dust into the eyes of an English plenipotentiary.

CHAPTER III.

BORROWED PLUMES.

MEANTIME, we had not forgotten our old friend Moses.

The "Blue Anchor" was a music-hall before that kind of entertainment was supposed to be invented. That is to say, long before the name of mnsic was debased, and song dragged in the dust before London audiences of shop-boys and flashy gents, the thing was already flourishing in our seaport towns for the benefit of soldiers and sailors. The "Anchor," as it was lovingly called, stood in a crowded street, where every second house was a beershop, and the house between a pawnbroker's. It had a parterre, or pit, the entrance to which was free, where Jack the Sailor, Joe the Marine, and the

Boiled Lobster could sit in comfort and dignity, each man with his pipe in his mouth and his pot before him.   It was a long, high, and narrow room. At the end stood a platform, where the performances took place, and under the platform, just as you may see in the present London houses, was a table where the proprietor, acting as Chairman, announced the songs and dances, called order, and superintended the comfort of his guests.   A small and select band of admirers rallied round the Chairman, and were privileged not only to call for drinks to assuage the great man's thirst, but also from time to time to take the hammer of authority.   At the other end of the hall was a small gallery, where young naval officers and subalterns sometimes honoured the representations by their appearance. It was to this gallery that we repaired, Leonard and I, accompanied by a second lieutenant of the Navy.   He was a cheerful youth, of smiling demeanour, whose chief merit in my eyes was his unbounded admiration for Leonard.   He met us by accident, and volunteered to join us, not knowing the nature of our quest ; on being informed that there might be a row, he became the more eager to

come with us. The fervent prayer of every young
naval officer on every possible occasion that there
may be a row is surely a healthy distinguishing
characteristic of the Navy. Certainly the members
of no other service or profession with which I am
acquainted are desirous of a fight on any possible
occasion.

We went, therefore, into the gallery, where there
were a dozen of noisy middies and young naval
fellows, who had been dining not wisely, but too
well.

There was an interval in the performance, and a
buzz of conversation going on. Now and then one
of the audience would lift up his voice with a snatch
of a chorus, to be taken up by his neighbours, or,
if it was a favourite, by the whole audience.

· We looked about the room. No Moses had
arrived yet. That was quite certain. Because
from our gallery we could see everybody in the
hall, and there was no doubt about our recognising
Moses—so old a friend.

We sat down in the front row and looked on.

Down came the hammer, with some inaudible
remarks from the Chair. There was silence for a

moment, and then a shout, not of applause, but of derision, as a man, dressed in sailor rig, bounded on the stage, and began to dance a hornpipe.

"Where was you shipped, mate?" "When was you last paid off?" There was no denying the dance, which was faithfully executed, but in consequence of the absence of some professional detail, probably in the dancer's get-up, the sailors with one consent refused to recognise him as a brother. The row grew tremendous as the performer went on, resolutely refusing to recognise any objection raised to his personal appearance. At last a stalwart young fellow bounded from a table in the auditorium to the platform, coolly hustled the professional with a hitch or two of his shoulder off the stage, and proceeded to execute the hornpipe himself, amid the exclamations of his comrades and brethren of the sister services. The band, consisting of two fiddles, a harp, and a cornet, went on playing steadily, whatever happened in the house. It was like Wassielewski, fiddling while the sailors sung, drank, and danced—himself unregarding.

The dance over, and the applause subsided, the

young fellow jumped back to his place, and down came the Chairman's knocker again. Sam Trolloper, he announced, this time—without any prefix or handle to the name, as if one would say Charles Dickens, or Julius Cæsar—was about to sing the Song of the Day.

The illustrious Sam, who was a popular favourite, and received the vociferous applause as something due to real merit, appeared in a suit of shore-going togs. He wore a coat all tails, with a hat all brim, and trousers of which one leg was gone, and the other going. Boots without socks, a ragged shirt, and a red kerchief tied around his neck, completed a garb, which, coupled with the fellow's face of low cunning and inextinguishable drollery, made him up into as complete an habitual criminal as you are likely to meet outside of Short's Gardens. He brandished a short stick, with a short preliminary walk across the stage, and then began the following :

> "'Tis O ! for a gay and a gallant bark,
>   A brisk and a lively breeze,
>   A bully crew and a captain too,
>   To carry me o'er the seas.

To carry me o'er the seas, my boys,
　To my own true love so gay,
　　For she's taking of a trip
　　In a Government ship,
　Ten thousand miles away.
　　　　Then blow, ye winds, heigho !
　　　　For a roaming we will go,
　　　I'll stay no more on England's shore ;
　　　　Then let the music play,
　　　For I'm off by the morning train
　　　Across the raging main,
　　I'm on the rove to my own true love,
　　Ten thousand miles away.

" My true love she was beautiful,
　My true love she was fair,
Her eyes were blue as the violets true,
　And crimson was her hair,
And crimson was her hair, my boys,
　But while I sing this lay
　　She's doing of the grand
　　In a distant land,
Ten thousand miles away.

" The sun may shine through a London fog,
　The Thames run bright and clear,
The ocean brine may turn to wine
　Ere I forget my dear.
Ere I forget my dear, my boys,
　The landlord his quarter day,
　　For I never can forget
　　My own dear pet,
Ten thousand miles away.

"Oh ! dark and dismal was the day
    When last I saw my Meg,
  She'd a Government band around each hand,
    Another one round each leg.
Another one round each leg, my boys,
    Dressed all in a suit of grey,
      ' My love,' said she,
      ' Remember me,
    Ten thousand miles away.'

" Oh ! would I were a bo's'n tight,
    Or e'en a bombardier ;
  I'd hurry afloat in an open boat,
    And to my true love steer.
And to my true love steer, my boys,
    Where the dancing dolphins play,
      And the shrimps and the sharks
      Are a having of their larks
  Ten thousand miles away.
        Then blow, ye winds, heigho !
        For a roaming we will go,
    I'll stay no more on England's shore ;
        Then let the music play,
      For I'm off by the morning train
      Across the raging main,
    I'm on the rove to my own true love,
      Ten thousand miles away."

This ditty, which the singer gave with a rich
rollicking baritone, and in a rolling tune, was
accompanied by a chorus from a couple of hundred

throats, which made the windows rattle and the glasses vibrate. Such a chorus, all bawling in unison, I never heard before. When the last bars, affectionately clung to by voices loth to let them go, died away, the illustrious Sam had disappeared, only to emerge again in a new disguise and sing another song. But, as the hammer fell to announce his return, Leonard touched my arm, and I saw our old friend Moses walking grandly among the chairs in the direction of the President.

I had not seen him for more than twelve years, but there was no mistaking his identity. It was the same dear old Moses. There was no real change in him ; only a development of the well-known boyish graces. The blotches upon his fat and bloated face ; the swagger with which he swung along the room ; the hat cocked on one side of his head ; the short stick carried half in the side pocket of his coat ; the flashy rings upon his fingers ; the gaudy necktie ; and the loud pattern of his trousers ;—all seemed part and parcel of the original Moses. He was only the infant Moses grown up ; Mrs. Jeram's Moses expanded, according to the immutable laws of

Nature, which allow of no sudden break, but only a wavy line of continuity. Selfish, greedy, and unscrupulous he had been as a child, just such he appeared now. Was it education alone, I thought, which made the difference between him and Leonard? It could hardly be that, because there was Jem Hex, himself as good a fellow as ever piped all hands, to set on the other side. Leonard! For a moment he stood irresolute, his hands clenched, just as he used to look in the days of old before he "went for" Moses. He waited till he saw his enemy seated by the Chairman. Then he touched my arm, and strode across the benches of the gallery to the door. I followed, and so did our friend the Navy man. We got downstairs and followed Leonard closely as he marched, head erect and with flashing eyes, straight up the hall.

There was a little commotion among the soldiers at sight of him.

"Gentleman Jack," the men whispered to each other. Leonard took no notice. One or two of them stood up to salute him. "Three cheers for Gentleman Jack and the Rifle-pit," shouted an enthusiastic private of his regiment. Everybody knew about the Rifle-pit, and the cheering was taken up with a will. Leonard stopped for a moment and looked round. When the cheers ceased he held up his hand and nodded. Three times three. The music, meantime, went on, and the singer made no pause. It was the illustrious Sam again—this time in the disguise of a soldier— supposed to be in liquor, and suffering from the melancholy of a love disappointment, as appeared from the only two lines of the song which I heard :

> " There I see the faithless she,
>   A cooking sausages for he."

But the attention of the audience was at this point wholly distracted from the singer. The Chairman and the band alone paid attention to him : these were of course professionally engrossed in admiration of the performance. For two circum- stances, besides the cheering for Leonard, and both of an agreeable and pleasing character, happened at this juncture to call away the thoughts of the men from imaginary sorrows. The first was that the middies in the gallery, having succeeded in hooking up a soldier's cap by means of a string and a pin, were now hauling away at their line, while the owner vainly imprecated wrath below. To join common cause with a comrade is the first duty of a soldier. A dozen men instantly jumped upon the tables, and a brief parley, in which strong words were answered with gentle chaff, was followed by a storm of pewter pots, whose battered sides indicated that they had before this hurtled through the air on a similar occasion. The middies instantly ducked, and the shower of projectiles passed as harmlessly over their heads as a cannonade at a modern siege. The storm having ceased, one middy, cautiously peeping over the gallery, seized the moment of comparative calm and hurled a pewter back. Instantly another and a fiercer hail of pint-pots. These having ceased, the middies swiftly creep over the seats and skedaddle, heaving over a spare half-dozen ere they reach the portals and fly down the stairs. When the brave redcoats have swarmed up the eight feet pillars and stormed the gallery, they found it like another Malakoff—empty. Then they shout. Who can withstand the bravery of the British soldier? All this takes time and attracts attention. Meantime, another scene is enacted at our end of the hall.

Leonard stalking up the room, the red-jackets shouting for " Gentleman Jack," the curiosity of those who do not know him, draw upon us the eyes of our old enemy, Moses. He knows us instantly, and with a hasty gesture to the Chairman, whose glass he has just filled, he rises, to effect a retreat by way of the orchestra and under the stage-door. Not so fast, friend Moses. Leonard makes for him ; there is a cry, and the pretender to the name of Copleston is dragged back to the table by the coat-collar. " Now—you—whatever you call your-self," cries Leonard, " what do you mean by taking my name ?"

" Let me go." Moses wriggles under the grasp which held him by the coat-collar like a vice, and drags him backwards upon the table among the glasses, where he lies like a turned turtle, feet up and hands sprawling, a very pitiable spectacle.

" Let me go, I say."

" Presently. Tell me your name."

" Moses Copleston," he replied, with an attempt at defiance.

" Liar !"

"Moses Copleston, oh! Won't any one help a fellow ?"

" Liar, again !"

" Let me get up, then."

Leonard let him rise, his friend the Lieutenant being the other side of the table, and a few of his own men having gathered round, so that there was little chance of the man's escape.

" What have I done to you now ?" whined Moses. " What have I done to you, I should like to know ? See here, Mr. Chairman of this respectable Free-and-Easy Harmonic Meeting, what did I say to him ? What did I do to him ? Here's a pretty go for a peaceable man to be set upon for nothing."

" Why have you dared to take my name," cried Leonard—" to drag into police courts and prisons ?"

" Your name ? O Lord ! *His* name ! What a thing to take ! Which he was born in Victory Row, and his mother——"

Here a straight one from the left floored Moses, and he fell supine among the chairs, not daring to arise.

The Lieutenant picked him up, and placed him—because he declined to stand : and, indeed, the claret was flowing freely—in the President's armchair.

"Yar—yar !" he moaned. "Hit a man when he is down. Hit your own brother. Yar !—Cain—Cain—Cain and Abel ! Hit your own twin brother."

" Liar, again," said Leonard, calmly. " Do you see any likeness, Grif,"—Grif was the *sobriquet* of the young sailor—" between me and this—this cur and cad ?"

" Can't say I do, old man."

" He has taken my name ; he has traded on it ; by representing himself to be—my mother's son—he has obtained from some one, money to spend in drink. I do not know who that person is. But I mean to know."

" Ho ! ho !" laughed Moses, mopping up the blood. " Can't hit a man when he's down. Yar ! Shan't get up. Wouldn't he like to know, then ? Ho ! Ho !"

" Get policeman," said Grif. " Follow him up and down."

" Beg pardon, sir," said one of the men, saluting Leonard, " best search his pockets."

Moses turned pale and buttoned up his coat.

" That seems sound advice, Leonard," I said. " Sit down, and let the men do it for you."

Well—it was a strange performance in an Harmonic meeting, but it attracted considerable attention, much more than the ditty which it interrupted ; as much as the flight of pewters backwards and forwards in the lower end of the gallery

They told off four, under a corporal, and then they seized the unhappy Moses. First the Chairman said he would turn down the lights, but was persuaded by Grif, not without a little gentle violence, to sit down comfortably, and see fair play. Then the orchestra left off playing to see this novelty in rows, a thing they hadn't done, except in the daytime and on Sundays, for twenty years. Then the Illustrious Baritone, Sam, himself came down from the stage to witness the scene. And, but for the kicks, the struggles, the many unrighteous words used by the victim, one might have thought that it was the unrolling by a group of *savans* of an Egyptian mummy.

First they took off his coat.   It contained, in his pockets, the following articles :

    1. A "twopenny smoke," so described by the Corporal.

    2. A pipe constructed of sham meerschaum.

    3. A box of fusees.

    4. The portrait of a young lady (daguerreotype) in *dégagée* costume.

    5. A penknife.

    6. Three pawnbrokers' tickets.

    7. A small instrument which, the Corporal suggested, was probably designed to pick locks with.

    8. Another "twopenny smoke."

    9. A sixpenny song book, containing one hundred sprightly ballads.

There was nothing else in the coat, but I was certain something would follow, because I had noticed the man's sudden pallor when the operation was suggested.

They next removed his waistcoat.

In the pockets were :

    1. A pipe poker.

    2. A quantity of loose tobacco.

3. Another "twopenny smoke," a little broken in the back.

4. Another box of fusees.

5. More pawnbrokers' tickets.

6. The sum of six shillings and twopence.

That was all, but on my taking the garment, I felt something rustle.

There was an inside pocket to the waistcoat. And in this—Moses made a frantic plunge—I found two letters. One, in a lady's handwriting, was addressed to Mr. Copleston, Post Office, to be called for; the other, in what may be best described as not a lady's hand, addressed to Miss Rutherford, Fareham. Now, Fareham is a small town at the upper end of the harbour. These letters I handed to Leonard. He read the address and put them in his pocket.

"Miss Rutherford," he repeated, with a strange light in his eyes.

Moses had recourse to violent language.

"Beg your pardon, sir," said the Corporal. "What to do next?"

"Let him go," said Leonard. "Or—stay—put him outside the place—but gently."

"Ah!—Yah!" Moses bellowed, bursting into what seemed a real fit of weeping. "This is the way that a twin brother behaves—this is getting up in the world."

"He is no brother of mine," said Leonard. "Come, Laddy—come, Grif."

The soldiers, when the weeping Moses had resumed his coat and waistcoat, ran him down the hall in quick and soldier-like fashion. As he was being run out, the orchestra played half-a-dozen bars of the Rogue's March, which was, under the circumstances, really a kindness, as it confirmed the minds of any possible waverers as to the iniquity of the culprit.

All was quiet again ; the pewter pots were being collected by a barman in the gallery; the noisy middies were gone ; the soldiers were sitting down again, and Moses received undivided attention as he was escorted to the doors.

Down went the Chairman's hammer.

"Gentlemen ! Sam Trolloper will again oblige."

Twang, fiddle ; blow, horn ; strike up, harp.

We went away as the orchestra played the opening to the accompaniment, and as the Illustrious Sam began a ballad of which we only heard the first two lines:

"As I sat by the side of the bubbling water
Toasting a herring red for tea."

CHAPTER IV.

MORE UNPLEASANTNESS FOR PERKIN WARBECK.

GRIF, greatly marvelling, went his own way, and Leonard, seizing my arm, hurried me home.

The Captain was gone to bed; we lit the lamp in the little parlour, and Leonard tore open the two letters with impatience.

That from Moses, ill spelt, ill conditioned, in a tone half bullying, half crawling, asked, as might be expected, for money. It was evidently not the first of such letters. It referred to his previous communications and interviews, appealed to his correspondent's close relationship, and went on to threaten, in case the money was not forthcoming, to do something vague but dreadful, which would bring him within the power of the law, in which

.case, he hinted, he should, from his commanding position in the dock, let all the world know that he had been driven to perpetrate the desperate deed by the obdurate and unrelenting heart of his own mother's sister, who rolled in gold and would give him none of it.

"There's a pretty villain for you," said Leonard, reading the last words with a clenched fist.

"I wish to go Strate," wrote Moses, in conclusion,. "as I have always gone Strate. If I am drove to go kruked there shan't be no one as shan't know it was Misery and your kruelty as done it. I must have a tenner to-morrow or the Day after if you've got to pawn your best black silk dress. Take and pawn it. Isn't that your Dooty? You in silk and me in rags and tatters. Why it make a cove sick to think of it. There. And specially a cove as is in-nercent, and one as has only got his karakter behind his back to depend upon—which the Lord He knows is a good one. So no more for the present from your affeckshunate nevew, Moses. P.S. Mind, I want the money right down. P.S. I know a most respectible pawnbroker and will call for the gownd myself. P.S. I am thinkin if it would be pleasant for you to have me at home always with you. Aunts and nevews oughter not to be sepperated."

"There's a precious villain for you," repeated Leonard, banging the table with his fist.

The other letter, to which this delightful epistle was apparently in reply, was written in expostulation of the man's extravagance and profligate habits. Evidently the writer was a lady. She spoke of her own small income; of the poverty in which she had to live in order to meet the demands which this fellow was perpetually making upon her; she had reminded him that he had drawn a hundred and fifty pounds out of her already; from which we inferred that the claims were comparatively recent; that she lived in daily terror of great demands; that she implored him to endeavour in some honourable way to get his own livelihood; and that his conduct and extravagance were causing her daily wretchedness—a letter which ought to have melted the heart even of a Moses. One thought, however, of the way in which that boy used to walk up all the jam, and felt sure that nothing would melt his granite heart.

"Laddy," cried Leonard. "Think! That fellow

may be even now on his way to make a final attempt upon this poor lady—my mother's sister—
my poor mother's sister."

His eyes filled with tears for a moment and his
voice choked.

"On the very day," he went on, "that Celia has
promised to be my wife, I am restored to my own
people. I cannot wait till to-morrow. Come with
me, Laddy, if you will—or I will go alone—I cannot rest. I shall go over to Fareham now, to-night
—if only to protect her from that fellow. Good
heavens! And he has got half-an-hour's start."

"He will walk," I said. ".We will go into the
town. It is only half-past nine. Get a dog-cart,
and drive over. We can easily get there before
him."

"He had a few shillings," Leonard reflected. "It is
not likely that he will spend them in driving. And
yet he knows it is his only chance to see her to-
night. If you cross the harbour first it is only six
miles to walk. Of course he will walk. By road it
is eleven miles. We can do it in an hour and
a half. Come, Laddy. Quick!"

It was easy enough to get a dog-cart, and in ten

minutes we were bowling along the road, Leonard driving something like Jehu.

He did not speak one word all the journey until we saw the lights of the little town in the distance. Then he turned his head to me and said quietly,

"I wonder what she will be like."

We clattered over the rough stones of the street, and stopped at the inn, where we had the horse taken out. The ostler undertook to guide us to Miss Rutherford's cottage.

It was nearly eleven o'clock, and most of the lights in the town were put out. For economy's sake the gas in the streets was not lit at all during this time of the year. We followed our guide down the street and beyond the houses, where began that fringe of small villa residences which is common to our English country towns, and distinguishes them especially from all continental towns. Stopping in front of one of these, our friendly ostler pointed to the garden gate.

"That's Miss Rutherford's, gentlemen. But you'll have to ring her up if you want to see the lady very particular, and to-night, because they're all gone to bed."

It was true. The house was dark, and its occupants probably asleep.

The ostler retraced his steps. We looked at each
other in dismay.

"I feel rather foolish," said Leonard. "We can't
very well knock at the door and wake up the poor
lady."

"Moses will probably have fewer scruples if he
arrives to-night on his private and very urgent
business."

"Yes ; that is true. Look here, Laddy, you go
back to the inn, and get a bed there. I will stay
outside, and watch here all night till the fellow
comes."

I would not consent to that. It seemed to me
fair that we should each do our turn of watching.

All this time we were standing outside the garden
gate. Within—one could see everything perfectly in
the midsummer twilight—was a trim and neat lawn,
set with standard roses and dainty flower-beds. Behind, a small house with a gable, round whose front
there climbed Westeria and passion-flower. The air
was heavy with the scent of the former. A lilac
was in full blossom among the shrubs, and added its

fresh spring-like perfume to the heavy odour of the creeper.

"It is all very peaceful," whispered Leonard. "Let us go inside and sit down."

We opened the gate, and stepped in as softly as a pair of burglars. On the right was a garden seat, over which drooped the branches of a laburnum. There we sat, expectant of Moses.

"I wonder what she is like," Leonard said again. "How shall we tell her? You must tell her, Laddy. And what will she tell me?

"It will be something more for Celia," he went on, "that her husband will have relations and belongings. It is too absurd to marry a man without even a cousin to his back. I have been ashamed all my life, not so much that I was born—as I was—as that I had no belongings at all. I used to envy, when I was a boy, the family life that we saw so little of—the mothers and sisters, the home-comings and the rejoicings—all the things one reads of in novels. We had none of these—except at second-hand, through Cis. You were better off than I, Laddy, because no one could take away your ancestry, though the compassionate

Czar relieved you of the burden of your wealth. But I had nothing. And now—what am I going to have ?

"She was good, my poor mother. So much Mrs. Jeram knows of her. But her mind wandered, and she could not, if she wished, have told her who or what she was. She was good, of that I am quite certain. But what about my father ?"

I made no reply. Within the sleeping house lay the secret. We had to pass the night before we could get at it. Perhaps, when it was found, poor Leonard would be no happier.

Twelve o'clock struck from some church tower near at hand. I thought of the night but a few weeks ago, when Celia and I sat whispering through the twilight hours in the stern of the boat. Well, he had come, of whom we talked that night ; he was with us ; he had told Celia that he loved her. It was quite certain what answer she would give her elderly suitor. Celia's father, besides, had got the key of the safe, the thing by which he declared he would rid himself at once of his persecutor. I had done that with Forty-four. Oh ! guilty pair. Was little Forty-four lying sleepless and remorseful on a conscience-stricken pillow? I, for my own part, felt small and rather mean thinking over what I had done—and how I had done it—but perhaps the "small" feeling was due rather to the knowledge how pitiably small we should look if we were found out. I believe that repentance generally does mean fear of being found out, when it does not mean the keener pang of intense disgust at having been actually exposed, in which case we call it Remorse. Borrowing that key for those few minutes, and setting the door of the safe open, was, as Mr. John Pontifex would have said, shaking his head and forefinger, a Wrong Thing, a thing to lament, as awful an event as his own profane language over the tough goose when in the full vigour and animal passion of his youth. And yet —and yet—one could not but chuckle over the thought of Herr Räumer's astonishment when he found the safe open and his victim free.

There was too much to think about as we sat beneath the laburnum in that quiet garden. Behind the forms of Celia and Leonard, behind the orange blossoms and flowers, rose a gaunt and weird figure, with a look of hungry longing in its

eyes, which were yet like the eyes of Wassielewski.
It reached out long arms and great bony hands
dripping with blood to seize me. And a mocking
voice cried, "Revenge thy father! revenge thy
father!" My brain reeled as thin shadows of
things, real and unreal, flitted across my closed
eyes. I awoke with a start.

One o'clock.

And just then we heard in the distance the
crunch of slow steps over the gravel of the road.

"Moses," Leonard whispered, springing into
attention.

The steps came nearer; they were a hundred
yards off; they were on the other side of the
hedge; they stopped at the garden wall.

"Moses," whispered Leonard, again.

It was Moses. And Moses in very bad temper.
He swore aloud at the garden-gate because he
could not at first find the handle. Then he
swore aloud in general terms, then he swore at
the people of the house because he would have
to ring them up, and then he came in banging
the door after him, and tramped heavily upon
the grass—the brute—crunching straight through

the flower-beds, setting his great heavy feet as if by deliberate choice on the delicate flowers. We were invisible beneath the laburnum tree.

Leonard rose noiselessly, and stepped after him.

See, another step, and he will be at the door, ringing the bell, terrifying out of their wits the women sleeping within. Already, as his scowling face shows in the twilight, he has formulated his requisition in his own mind, and is going to back it with threats of violence. The demands will never be made. The threats will never be uttered. Leonard's hand falls upon his shoulder, and Moses, turning with a start and a cry, finds himself face to face again with his old enemy.

"Come out of this garden," said Leonard. "Dare to say one word above your breath, and——"

Moses trembled, but obeyed. It was like Neptune's "Quos ego——"

Leonard dragged him, unresisting, into the road, and led him along the silent way, beyond earshot of the house, saying nothing.

"What shall we do to him?" he asked me.

"Oh! Mr. Ladislas," whimpered Moses, "don't let him murder me. You're witness that I never done nothink to him. Always hard on a poor innocent cove, he was, when we were all boys together."

"You came out to-night," said Leonard, "thinking you were going to find an unprotected woman asleep in the dead of night; you were persuading yourself that you would frighten her into giving you more money, knowing that it was your last chance."

"No, sir," whined Moses abjectly. "No, Captain Copleston, sir. Not that. What I said to myself, as I came along, was this : ' Moses,' I says, says I, 'the plant's found out. All is up. That's where it is.' So I says to myself—if you don't mind, sir, takin' your fingers from off o' my coat-collar, which they have a throttlesome feel"— Leonard released him. "Thank you, sir. I says to myself, then, ' I'll up and go to Miss Rutherford —which she is a generous-'earted lady, and tell her —tell her—Hall.' That's wot I meant to do, Cap'en Copleston, sir. Hall I was a-goin' to tell her."

"A likely story, indeed," said Leonard.

"Very likely, sir," Moses echoed. "Yes, and I should have said——"

"Now—you—drunken blackguard and liar," said Leonard, "you have come here to make a final attempt. You have failed. Henceforth, you will be watched. I give you fair warning that if you are ever seen by me about this place, or in any other place, I will instantly give you into custody on a charge of obtaining money on false pretences. You understand so much. Then go— get out of my sight."

He accompanied his words with a gesture so threatening that our prisoner instantly set off running as hard as he could down the road. If fear ever lent wings to a fugitive, those wings were produced for Moses on this occasion.

"I was in such a rage," said Leonard, as the steps died away in the distance, "such a boiling rage with the creature that I think I should have killed him had I not let him go. It is too bad, because he richly deserved the best cowhiding one could give him. Odd! All the old feeling came back upon me, too. I used to hate him in the old days when we fought night and morning. And I hate him now."

"What is to be done next?" I asked. "Are we to go back to the friendly laburnum? There is no fear about Moses any more."

"No; I don't care what we do. I am restless and excited. I cannot sleep. Perhaps she gets up early. Let us go for a walk."

Half-past one in the morning was rather late for an evening walk, but I complied, and we went along the deserted road. Presently I began to feel tired, and was fain to rest in the hedge under a tree. And there I fell fast asleep. When I awoke it was broad daylight. Leonard was walking backwards and forwards along the road. What a handsome man he was as he came swiftly towards me, bathed in the early sunshine which played in his curly hair, and lay in his eyes.

"Awake already, Laddy?" he cried. "It is only four o'clock. I am less sleepy than ever. And there are two long hours to wait. She can't get up before six. Perhaps she will not be up before nine."

I confess that those two hours were long ones.

Leonard's restless excitement increased. I made him walk. I made him bathe. I tried to make him talk, and yet the minutes crawled. At last, however, it was half-past six, and we retraced our steps to the cottage.

CHAPTER V.

MISS RUTHERFORD.

MISS RUTHERFORD was already up. At least a lady about five-and-forty, small, fragile, and dainty, with delicate features and an air of perfect ladyhood ; she wore a morning dress of muslin, with garden-gloves and a straw hat. And she was gazing with dismay at the footprints—that brute Moses !—on her flower-beds.

We looked at her for a few moments, and then Leonard opened the garden-gate, and we presented ourselves.

At least I presented both of us.

" Miss Rutherford,"—she looked surprised. " I am speaking to——Miss Rutherford, am I not ?"

" Yes. I am Miss Rutherford."

"We have something to tell you of importance. Will you take us into your house?"

She looked from one to the other.

"It is very early," she said. "My servants are not down yet—but come—you appear to be gentlemen."

She led the way to a little drawing-room, which was a mere bower of daintiness, the pleasant and pretty room of a refined and cultivated lady, with books and pictures, and all sorts of pretty things— fancy the hulking Moses in such an apartment!— and offered us chairs. There was nothing in the room which pointed to the presence of the sterner and heavier sex. Even the chairs seemed only calculated for ladies of her own slender dimensions. Leonard's creaked ominously when he sat down.

"Let me go back twenty-three years," I began. " but first I must tell you that my name is Ladislas Pulaski—here is my card—and that we do not come here from any idle motives. This gentleman—but you will see presently who he is."

"Three-and-twenty years ago?" Miss Rutherford began to tremble. "That was when I lost my sister—and my nephew was born. You come about

him, I am sure. He has done something terrible
at last, that boy, I am afraid. Gentlemen, remember
under what bad influences my nephew's early life
was spent. If you have to accuse him of anything
wrong—remember that."

"Pray do not be alarmed," I went on. "Your
nephew's early influences were not so bad as you
think, and you will very likely see reason to be
proud of him."

She shook her head, as if that was a thing quite
beyond the reach of hope.

Leonard was looking at her with curious eyes
that grew softer as they rested on this gentlewoman's sweet face.

"Twenty-three years ago, your sister died. Would
it pain you too much, Miss Rutherford, if you would
tell us something about her?"

"The pain is in the recollection, rather than the
telling," she replied. "My poor sister married an
officer."

"His name was Leonard Copleston," I said.

"Yes—you knew him perhaps? She was only
eighteen—three years younger than myself—and
she knew nothing of the world—how should she,

living as she had done all her short life in our quiet
country vicarage? She thought the man she
married was as good as he was handsome. She
admired him for his bravery, for the stories he
could tell, for the skill with which he rode, shot,
and did everything, and for the winning way he
had. My father liked him for his manly character,
and because he was clever, and had read as well as
travelled and fought. And I believe I liked him
as much as my father did. There was never any
opposition made, and my poor dear was married
to him in our own church, and went away with him
on her eighteenth birthday."

She paused for a moment.

"He was not a good man," she went on; "he
was a very, very bad man. I hope God has forgiven
him all the trouble and misery he brought upon us,
but I find it very hard to forgive. My sister's
letters were happy and bright at first; gradually—I
thought it was my own fancy—they seemed to lose
the old joyous ring; and then they grew quite sad.
In those days we did not travel about as we can
now, and all we could do was to wait at home and
hope. Six months after her marriage she came

back to us. Oh! my poor dear, so changed, so altered. She who had been the happiest of girls and the blithest of creatures was wan and pale, with a scared and frightened look"—Leonard rose, and went to the window, where he remained, half hidden by the curtain—"such a look as an animal might have who had been ill-treated. She came unexpectedly and suddenly, without any letter or warning—on a cold and snowy December afternoon : she burst into passionate weeping when she fell upon my neck; and she would never tell me why she left her husband. Nor would she tell my father.

"He began to write to her. She grew faint and sick when the first letter came; she even refused at first to read it; but she yielded, and he kept on writing; and one day, she told me that she had forgiven her husband, and was going back to him.

"She went. She went away from us with sad forebodings, I knew; she wrote one or two letters to us; and then—then we heard no more."

"Heard no more ?"

"No; we heard nothing more of her from that day. My father made inquiries, and learned that

Captain Copleston had left the army, sold out, and was gone away from the country—no one knew whither. His own family, we learned for the first time, had entirely given him up as irreclaimable, and could tell us no more. We heard nothing further, and could only conjecture that the ship in which they sailed had gone down with all on board. But why did she not write to tell us that she was going?

"We waited and waited, hoping against hope. And then we resigned ourselves to the conviction that she was dead. The years passed on; my father died, full of years, and I was left alone in the world. And then, one day last year, a letter came to me from America. It was a letter dictated by my sister's husband on his deathbed——"

"He is dead then? Thank GOD!" Was that the voice of Leonard, so hoarse, so thick with trouble?

"He implored my forgiveness, and that of his wife if she still lived. He confessed that he had let her go away—driven her away by his conduct, he said—when she was actually expecting to be confined, and that in order to begin life again without any ties he had emigrated. The letter was unfinished, because Death took him while he was still dictating it. Yet it brought me the comfort of knowing that he had repented."

"And then——," I asked, because she stopped.

" Then I began again to think of my poor sister, and I advertised in our two papers, asking if any one could give me tidings of her. For a long time I received no reply, but an answer came at last ; it was from my nephew, that unhappy boy, who seems to have inherited all his father's vices and none of his graces."

Poor Leonard ! What a heritage !

" It was from him that I learned how his mother— poor thing, poor thing!—died in giving birth to him : he told me that he had been brought up in a rough way, among soldiers and sailors ; that he knew nothing about any of his relations, that, as his letter would show me, he had little education, that he was a plumber and joiner by trade; and that by my help, if I would help him, he hoped to do well. In answer to his letter I made an appointment, and came down to meet him. I can hardly tell you what a disappointment it was to find my poor dear sister's son so rough and coarse. However, it was my duty to do what I could, and I moved down here in order to be near him, and help him to the best purpose."

She stopped and wiped away a tear.

"I have not been able to help him much as yet," she went on. "He is, indeed, the great trouble of my life. He has deceived me in everything; I find that he has no trade, or, at least, that he will not work at it; he said he had a wife and young family, and I have found that he is unmarried; he said he was a total abstainer—and—oh! dear me, he has been frequently here in a dreadful state of intoxication : he said he was a church-goer and a communicant.—But these things cannot interest you."

She said this a little wistfully, as if she hoped they might.

"They do interest us very much," I said.

"After all, he is my nephew," as if she could say much more, but refrained from the respect due to kinship.

"You have been deceived," I told her. "You have been very grossly deceived."

"I have," she said. "But I must bear with it."

"You have been deceived, madam, in a much more important way than you think. Listen to a little story that I have to tell you.

" There were once four boys living together in the house he showed you, all under the charge of an excellent and charitable woman named Mrs. Jeram, to whom we shall take you. One of these boys, the best of them all, was your nephew."

" The best of them all?" she repeated, bitterly. " Then what were the others like !"

"One of them, to whom I can also take you, was named James Hex. He is now a boatswain in the Royal Navy, a very good boatswain, too, I believe, and a credit to the service. Another was —myself."

" You ?"

" I, Miss Rutherford. I was placed there by my countrymen the Poles, with this Mrs. Jeram, and maintained by them out of their poverty. When one of these boys, your nephew, was eight or nine, and I a year or two younger, we were taken away from the good woman with whom we lived by a gentleman whom you shall very soon know. He adopted us, and had us properly educated."

"Properly educated? But my nephew can hardly write."

"Your nephew writes as well as any other gentleman in England."

"Gentleman in England?"

"My dear lady, the man who calls himself Moses Copleston is not your nephew at all. He was the fourth of those boys of whom I told you. He is the one among them who has turned out badly. He knew, no doubt from Mrs. Jeram, all about your nephew's birth. What he told you, so far, was true. All the rest was pure invention. Did you ever, for instance, see any resemblance in him to your late sister?"

"To Lucy? Most certainly not."

"To his father?"

"Not in face. But he has his father's vices."

"So have, unfortunately, a good many men."

"But I cannot understand. He is not my nephew at all? Not my nephew? Can any man dare to be so wicked?"

It really was, as we reflected afterwards, a claim of great daring, quite worthy to be admitted among those of historical pretenders. Moses was another Perkin Warbeck.

"Most certainly not your nephew. He is an impudent pretender. I do not ask you to accept my word only. I will give you proof that will satisfy any lawyer, if you please. He must have seen your advertisement, and knowing that the real nephew was gone away, devised the excellent scheme of lies and robbery, of which you have been the victim. Last night we wrung the truth from him ; last night he came here, to this house, intending to make a last attempt at extortion, but we were here before him. Your house was guarded for you all night—by your real nephew."

She was trembling violently. She had forgotten the presence of Leonard, who stood in the window, silent.

"My nephew? My nephew? But where is he? And oh! is he like that other? Is there more shame and wickedness ?"

"No! No shame at all. Only pride and joy. He is here, Miss Rutherford. See! This is Leonard Copleston, your sister's son."

Leonard stepped before her.

42—2

"I am, indeed," he said. "I am your sister's son."

What was it, in his voice, in his manner, in his attitude, that carried my thoughts backward with a rush to the day when he stood amid the snow in the old churchyard, and cried aloud to the spirit of his dead mother lying in the pauper's corner?

And was she like her dead sister, this delicate and fragile lady who must once have been beautiful, and who now stood with hands tightly clasped, gazing with trembling wonder on the gallant young fellow before her?

"My nephew?" she cried. "Leonard—it was your father's name—you have his hair and his eyes, but you have your mother's voice. Leonard, shall you love me?"

He took her two hands in his, and drew her towards him like a lover.

I thought they would be best left alone, and disappeared.

After meditation for a space among the flowers I went back again. They were still standing by the table, her hand in his. He held a miniature —I guessed of whom—and was looking on it with tearful eyes.

"Leonard," I said, " I shall take the dog-cart into town, and leave you with your aunt to tell your own story. Bring her with you this very afternoon, and introduce her to the Captain. Miss Rutherford, you are pleased with this new nephew of yours?"

"Pleased?" she cried with a sob of happiness. " Pleased?"

"He is an improvement upon the old one. Moses, indeed! As if you could have a nephew named Moses, with a drink-sodden face and a passion for pipes and beer!"

She laughed. The situation had all the elements of tears, and I wanted to stave them off.

"And then there is Celia," I added.

"Celia? Who is Celia?" she asked, with a little apprehension in her voice. "Are you married, my nephew, Leonard?"

"No," he said. "But I am in love."

"Oh!"

"And you will like her, Aunt."

They were strange to each other, and Leonard handled the title of relationship with awkwardness at first. It was actually the very first of those titles

—there are a good many of them when you come to think of them—that he had ever been able to use.

" Miss Rutherford must be prepared to fall in love with her," I said, to reassure her ; " everybody is in love with Celia."

Then I left them, and went back to the tavern, where I had breakfast—nothing gives a man such an appetite as these domestic emotions—and drove back to town.

CHAPTER VI.

A FAMILY COUNCIL.

LEONARD'S promotion to family connections was a thing so startling that it almost drove away from my mind the recollection of the crisis through which all our fortunes were to pass that very day— Celia's refusal of Herr Räumer and my Polish deputation. In the breathless rush of those two days, in which were concentrated the destinies of three lives at least, one had to think of one thing at a time. Fortunately, I could give the morning to Celia. She was agitated, but not on her own account. Her, father, she said, had given her his unqualified approval of what she was going to do.

"He has behaved," she said, "in the kindest way possible. He knows all about—about Leonard."

" I told him."

" And he says he is very glad. I am to meet
Herr Räumer at twelve in his office and give him
my answer. But there is something behind all this
which troubles me. Why is my father so sad ?"

" It is nothing at all, I believe. He fancies that
the German can injure his reputation in some way.
Be of good heart, Cis. All will go right now."

And then I fell to telling her how Leonard had
at last come into the patrimony of a family, and
was no longer a foundling. This diverted her
thoughts, and carried us on until twelve o'clock,
when I went to the family conference which was
called at that hour in Mr. Tyrrell's office. Celia
remained in her own room until she was wanted.

It was a complete assemblage, gathered together
to hear Celia's answer to her suitor. Nothing but
the gravity of the situation warranted this publicity,
so to speak, of her decision. It was an acknow-
ledgment, on the part of her father, that more was
at stake than the mere refusal of a girl to marry a
man old enough to be her grandfather. Mr. Pontifex was there also with his wife. He wore the
garb which he assumed on occasions of ceremony.

It consisted simply of a dress-coat, with perhaps an additional fold to the very large white neckcloth which he wore about his long neck. That dress-coat, which he certainly never associated especially with the evening, bore an air of battle about it, although the wearer's face was much meeker than usual, and his upper lip longer, and therefore sadder to look at. They sat each bolt upright in two chairs side by side against the wall. The lady was present under protest. As I heard afterwards, she consented to come on the express understanding that her carriage should be kept waiting, so that at any moment, if she were offended, she might go ; also, that the maintenance of her will on its present terms depended on Celia's behaviour. Her husband, the principal sufferer in their family disturbances, had, I suppose, received orders to be on distant terms with everybody, as if we were all on our trial. I gathered this from the way in which he acknowledged my presence, with that sort of dignified movement of the head which the clergy reserve for pew-openers, sextons, national school-masters, and the like. He was present at the meeting, perhaps, to represent the virtue of Christian resignation, while his wife preferred that Christian wrath the exhibition of which is not a sin.

Mrs. Tyrrell sat on the other side of the room in a state of profound bewilderment. Things were beyond her comprehension. But she seemed to feel my arrival as a kind of relief, and immediately proposed, as a measure of conciliation, wine and ·cake. No one took any notice of the offer except Mr. Pontifex, who sighed and shook his head as if he should have liked some under happier circumstances.

It was very evident that Aunt Jane thought she had been invited to witness the acceptance of the ·enemy's offer. There was in the carriage of her head, the setting of her lips, the rustle of her silks, the horizontality of her curls, a wrathful and combative look. And if her eyes seemed to wander, as they sometimes did, into space, it was, one instinctively felt, only the absorption of her spirit in the ·effort to find fitting words to express her indignation when the time should arrive.

I looked at the Safe. Yes, the door was slightly ·open ; I had left it wide open. There could be no doubt that Mr. Tyrrell had found it open. Presumably, therefore, he had——what had he done? Abstracted papers? The thought was an ugly one; and yet, for what other reason had I committed an ugly act and borrowed the key? Abstracted papers; made things safe; robbed his enemy of his weapons; that did not ring musically—as every musician knows, evil is discord. And yet, Mr. Tyrrell did not look like—one shrinks from calling things by their right names. He bore, on the other hand, a quiet look of dignity which contrasted strangely with the restless nervousness of the last few weeks.

With him was the Captain standing with his back to the fireplace, the favourite British position, summer or winter.

All these observations were made in a moment, for, as if he had been waiting for me, Mr. Tyrrell began to address us, fidgeting his fingers among the papers on the table.

"I have asked you to come here this morning," he said. "I have asked you, Aunt Jane and Mr. Pontifex, as Celia's nearest relations, and you, Captain, as an old friend, and you, Ladislas, as her closest friend, to witness her own decision in a matter which concerns her own happiness, what-ever we may have thought or said about it—and which must be left entirely to herself.

Mrs. Pontifex snorted.

"I keep my own opinion, George Tyrrell," she said, "and I mean to keep it."

"You all know that this offer took us entirely by surprise—none more so than myself—and espe-cially for the reason that its rejection by Celia will most likely result in the emnity of a man who has for many years been my friend and my client."

Here Mrs. Pontifex murmured in an undertone, so that her husband and I were the only persons who heard it :

"Fudge and flapdoodle."

"There was nothing against Herr Räumer. He has lived among us an irreproachable life, so far as we know."

"Old enough to be her grandfather; a foreigner; and, for all you know, a Roman Catholic."

John Pontifex lifted his head at the last word, and made a remark :

"That we should innocently connive at the marriage of an unfortunate Papist would be—ahem —in fact—a Shocking State of Things!"

"Of course he is not a Catholic," said Mr. Tyrrell, impatiently. "And as for his age, many girls marry elderly men and are perfectly happy. It so happens that eight or ten years ago I laid myself under an obligation—a very great obligation—to Herr Räumer. I cannot allow myself to forget the debt I owe him. At the time when I expressed my gratitude and asked in what way I could best show it, he laughed, and said that I could give him—my little daughter. I acceded, laughing, and thought no more about the matter until he himself reminded me of it. It seems that he had not forgotten it. At the same time, he offered to take his chance; if I would give him such good offices as I could, in the way of paternal influence; if I would give him opportunities of frequently seeing my daughter: if Mrs. Tyrrell could also be got to approve——"

"Nothing could be more regular, I must say," sighed Mrs. Tyrrell, "or more becoming."

Mrs. Pontifex pulled out her pocket-handkerchief

and coughed. I distinctly heard the last syllables, drowned by the kerchief—"doodle."

Her husband, terrified beyond measure by this repetition of his wife's very strongest expression, shook his head slowly, and ejaculated, Heaven knows why, " Alas !"

" I say," Mr. Tyrrell went on, mildly, disregarding these interruptions, " that he very properly left the decision to Celia herself. At first I considered the situation favourably for my old friend. Here was an establishment, a certainty, an assured position. I brought pressure—not cruel or unkind pressure—but still a certain amount of pressure—to bear upon Celia in his behalf. I am sorry now that I did exercise that influence, because it has offended some here, and because I find it has made my daughter unhappy, and that "—his voice broke down a little—" is a thing I cannot bear to think of.——

" Yesterday, however," he went on, after a pause, during which Mrs. Pontifex did not say, " Fudge and Flapdoodle," nor did her husband say, " Alas !" but looked straight before him—" Yesterday I saw Herr Räumer again ; he came to tell me that he

had waited two months, that Celia was now exposed to the attentions of a far younger and more
attractive man in the shape of Leonard Copleston,.
and that he would ask Celia himself at twelve to-
day for her decision. I have this morning talked
with her upon the subject. I have told her that I
withdraw altogether every word I said before in
favour of his pretensions ; I have asked her to be
guided in the matter entirely by her own heart.
And I invited you here, with her consent, in order
that, before you all, she might tell Herr Räumer
what answer she has decided to give."

"So far, George Tyrrell," said Mrs. Pontifex,.
"you have acted worthily, and like yourself."

Then the Captain lifted up his voice.

"Our friend, George Tyrrell," he began, "told
me yesterday a thing which has been hitherto
known only to himself and to this Mr.—Herr
Räumer. It is a matter which may, or may not,.
do harm if generally known. And it appears that
yesterday, probably in the heat of jealousy or disappointment—because we all know Celia Tyrrell's.
sentiments in the matter—this gentleman held out
a kind of threat against Celia's father of spreading·

the business abroad. We can afford to laugh at such menaces ; we stick to our guns, and we let the enemy blaze away. He cannot do us any real harm."

"Menaces ? Threats ?" cried Aunt Jane, springing to her feet, and shaking her skirts so that they "went off" in rustlings like a whole box of lucifer matches at once. "Threats against *you*, George Tyrrell? Against a member of *my* family? Threats? I'll let him know, if he begins that kind of thing. He shall see that I *can* be resolute on occasion, meek though I may be habitually and on Christian principle."

"Certainly, my dear," said John Pontifex, sadly. "You can be resolute on proper occasion."

George Tyrrell smiled—rather a wan smile.

"It is never pleasant to have one's peace and ease disturbed by threats and misrepresentations."

"We've got you in convoy," said the Captain, heartily ; "and will see you safe into port. There's eight bells. Now, then."

I was still thinking about the open safe. Could a man who had spoken as Tyrrell spoke, with so much genuine feeling, so much dignity, actually have in his pockets abstracted papers? Then why the undertone of melancholy? If he had nothing to fear, why did he speak or allow the Captain to speak of possible attacks? In any case, I was the real culprit, the cause and origin of the crime.

CHAPTER VII.

CELIA GIVES HER ANSWER.

WE had not long to wait. Almost as the last clock finished its last stroke of noon we heard outside the firm and heavy step of Celia's suitor, and I am ready to confess that the heart of one guilty person in the room—if there were more than one—began to beat the faster. Mr. Tyrrell turned pale, I thought, and Mrs. Pontifex stiffened her back against the chair, and looked her most resolute. I do not know why, but John Pontifex began to tremble at the knees, the most sensitive part apparently of his organisation.

Herr Räumer stood before us in some surprise.

"I did not expect," he said, "to find a *conseil de famille.*" Then drawing from the solemn aspect of

Mrs. Pontifex, the dejection depicted in Mrs.
Tyrrell's face, and the terror of John Pontifex, a
conclusion that the meeting was not favourable to
his cause, he assumed an expression which meant
fighting.

"I hope that Mrs. Pontifex is quite well," he
said, blandly, "and the Rev. Mr. Pontifex, whom I
have not heard for several Sundays."

Then he took a chair, and sat at the table.

"Now," he said to Mr. Tyrrell, with a certain
brutality, "let us get to business at once."

Beside him was the Captain, leaning his hand on
his stick, and looking as if he were ready with the
loaded artillery of a hundred-gun man-o'-war.

Mr. Tyrrell rang the bell.

"Ask Miss Celia to be good enough to step
down," he said. Whatever was before him he
looked ready to face.

The German, as if master of the situation, sat
easily and quietly. He looked as if he were a
mere spectator, and the business was one which
concerned him not at all. And yet he must have
known, from the fact of the family gathering, that
his chances were small indeed. But he said nothing,

only removed his blue spectacles, and gently stroked his heavy moustache with the palm of his left hand. He was dressed, I remember, in a white waistcoat, only the upper part being visible above his tightly-buttoned frock-coat. He wore a flower in one button-hole, which was then not so common as it is now, and a tiny piece of red ribbon in another. Also he wore lavender kid gloves and patent-leather boots. In fact, he was dressed for the occasion. With his heavy face, his large and massive head, his full moustache, and his upright carriage, he looked far younger, in spite of his white hair, than the man who sat expectant before him. Celia entered in her quiet, unobtrusive way, kissed her great-aunt, and, refusing a chair which Herr Räumer offered, took mine, which was next Aunt Jane.

"Now, Celia," said that lady, "we are all here, waiting for your decision, and as that may possibly —mind, child, I do not expect it—but it may possibly be such as John Pontifex and I cannot approve, the sooner we get it the better."

"One moment," said Herr Räumer, rising, and pushing back his chair. "I am also deeply concerned in Miss Tyrrell's answer. May I speak first?"

He considered a moment, and then went on.

"I am now a man advanced in years. I have for twelve years and more watched the growth of a child so carefully that I have at last, perhaps prematurely, come to look upon that child as, in a sense, my own. You would laugh, Mrs. Pontifex, if I were to say that I have fallen in love with that child."

"Fudge and flapdoodle!" said the lady for a third time, so that her husband's teeth began to chatter.

"Quite so. But it is the truth. I hope—I still venture to hope—that my declining years may be cheered by the care of a young lady, who, in becoming my wife, would not cease to be my much-loved and cherished daughter."

"Man," said Aunt Jane, "talk Christian sense, not heathen rubbish. You can't marry your daughter nor your granddaughter either. Not even in Germany, far less in this Protestant and Evangelical country."

"I went to my old friend, George Tyrrell," Herr

Räumer proceeded, regardless of the interruption, " I put the case before him. You know the rest. Celia, I have not pressed my attentions upon. you. I have said no word of love to you. I know that it might be ridiculous in me to say much of what I feel in this respect. You know me well enough to trust me, I think. It was enough for me that you should know what I hoped, and it was right that you should take time to reflect. Will you be my wife ?"

She clasped my hand, and held it tight. And she looked at her father with a little fear and doubt, while she answered,

" I cannot, Herr Räumer."

His face clouded over.

" Think," he pleaded. " I have watched over you, looking for this moment, for ten years. You shall have all that a woman can ask for. I can give you position—a far higher position than you dream of. You shall be rich, you shall be a guest of Courts, you shall lead and command—what *can* a woman want that I cannot give you ?"

She shook her head.

" I am very sorry, you have been very kind to me always."

"His attentions have been most marked," said her mother.

"Clara," said Aunt Jane, sharply, "hold your tongue!"

"You have been so kind to me always that I venture to ask one more kindness of you. It is that you forget this passage of your life altogether, and—and—do not suffer my refusal to alter the friendly relations between my father and yourself."

"Is this scene preconcerted?" he turned to Mr. Tyrrell. "Am I invited here to make one in a dramatic representation? Are these excellent friends gathered together to laugh at the refusal of my offer?"

"No—no," cried Celia. "There is no dramatic representation. There is no preconcerted scene. Come, Aunt Jane, come, mamma; let us go; we have nothing more to do here. Herr Räumer" —she held out her hand—"will you forgive me? I—I alone am to blame—if any one is to blame— in this matter. I ought to have told you three weeks ago that it was impossible. I hoped that you would see for yourself that it was impossible.

I thought that you would of your own accord withdraw your offer.   Will you forgive me ?"

He did not take the proffered hand.

" You refuse my hand," he said, " and you ask
me to take yours !   Pardon me, Miss Tyrrell.   We
do not fight with ladies.   I have now to do with
your father."

Mrs. Pontifex—I think I have said that she was
not a tall woman, being perhaps about five feet two
—stepped to the table, and rapped it smartly with
her knuckles.

" You have to do with Jane Pontifex," she said,
" as well as with George Tyrrell.   Take care.
John Pontifex !"

" My dear !"

" Remain here.   Watch the proceedings, and
report them to me, exactly.   Now, Clara and
Celia, go on upstairs.   You are under *my* protection
now, my dear.   And as for you, sir," she shook
her finger impressively at Herr Räumer, " if it were
not for your age and infirmities, I would take you
by the collar and give you as good a shaking as
you ever had.   John Pontifex !"

" My—my—my—dear ?"

"I charge you—*not* to shake him by the collar."

"No, my dear, I will not," he promised, firmly.

"In moments of indignation," Aunt Jane explained to her niece, "John Pontifex is like a lion."

She stood at the door to see Celia safely out of her suitor's clutches, and then followed, closing it with a slam.

John Pontifex, the Lion-hearted, resumed his seat against the wall, and sat bolt upright with more meekness than might have been expected of one so disposed to Christian wrath.

"Now, sir," said Herr Räumer to Mr. Tyrrell, "the she-dragon is gone, and we can talk—"

"I have promised, Johnny," whispered Mr. Pontifex to me, "not to shake him. By the she-dragon, I presume, he—actually—means—Mrs. Pontifex. This wickedness is, indeed, lamentable!"

"—— and we can talk. Is this bravado, or is it defiance?"

"It is neither," said the Captain. "I know all the particulars of this business. It means that we are doing our duty, and are prepared for the consequences."

"Ah!" said Herr Räumer. "It is very noble of you to recommend this line of action, seeing that the consequences will not fall upon your head. You are one of the people who go about enjoining everybody, like Nelson, to do his duty because England expects it. England is a great and a fortunate country."

"You may sneer, sir," said the Captain, with dignity. "I have told you what we propose to do."

"Are you aware what the consequences may be if I act upon certain information contained in that safe, that you so boldly recommend the path of duty?"

"I believe the consequences may be unpleasant. But they will be made quite as unpleasant to yourself; they cannot produce the important effects you anticipate; and—in any case—we shall abide the consequences."

"I give you another chance, Tyrrell. Let the girl give me a favourable answer in a week—a fortnight—even a month. Send young Copleston away—use your paternal pressure, and all may yet be well."

He had quite put off the bland politeness of his

manner with Celia, and stood before us angry, flushed, and revengeful. It was pretty clear that he would get what revenge he could, and I began to hope that, after all, Mr. Tyrrell *had* possessed himself of those papers.

"Come, Tyrrell," he said, "you know what will follow. Think of your own interests. I have never yet been beaten, and I never will. Those who stand in my path are trampled on without mercy."

"No," said the Worshipful the Mayor, "I will not be under any man's power. Do what you like, say what you like; and as you please. I would rather see Celia dead than married to you."

"Then you declare war?" he took a little key— ah! how well I remembered that instrument of Temptation — from his waistcoat-pocket. "You declare war? This is refreshing. Some people say that nothing will ever induce an Englishman to declare war again. And here we have an example to the contrary. But I must crush you, my friend. I really must crush you."

"Gad!" cried the Captain. "Can't you open fire without so much parley? We are waiting for your shot."

"Tyrrell"—Herr Räumer turned upon him once more—"I am almost sorry for you, and I have never been sorry for any one yet. Such a pity! The Worshipful the Mayor! The rich and prosperous lawyer! The close relative of the great Pontifex family! With so large a balance at the bank, and so many shares, and such an excellent business! And all to come to such a sudden and disagreeable end. It does seem a pity."

"Pluck up, Tyrrell! this is all bounce."

I wondered if it was. At that moment Mr. Tyrrell quietly went to the safe.

"I will not trouble you to open the safe. It is already open."

Herr Räumer sat down and looked at him.

"This is a stroke of genius," he said. "I did not think you had it in you. Were you, too, Captain, an accomplice? He finds my safe open, or he gets a key, or in some way opens it; he takes the compromising papers, and then, you see, in full family gathering he defies me. It is an excellent situation, well led up to, well contrived, and executed admirably. Tyrrell, you are a dramatist lost to your country."

He did not appear the least disconcerted; he took it as quite natural that he should be defeated by deceit, craft, and cunning; they were weapons which he held to be universal and legitimate; he had, as he might cynically say, used them himself all his life. Now, in an unexpected manner, he was actually met and defeated by his own methods.

"This is really refreshing. Who is the best man in all the town, Ladislas Pulaski? Is it George Tyrrell? Why, he is better than the best, because he is the cleverest."

"Perhaps not," said Mr. Tyrrell, as he took a bundle of papers tied in red tape out of the safe. "I found this open last night. I suppose you left it open. There are all your papers—untouched."

The German snatched them from his hands, and began to turn them over.

"All? All?" He untied the tape, and opened paper after paper. "All? Impossible." He looked carefully through the whole bundle. As he got to the end his face changed, and he looked bewildered. "They are all here," he said, looking at us with a sort of dismay. "What is the meaning of this?"

He sat down with the papers in his hands, as if he were facing a great and astonishing problem.

"You are a theologian, Mr. Pontifex, and have presumably studied some of the leading cases in what they call sin. Did you ever read of such a case as this?"

"When I was a young man at Oxford (where—ahem—I greatly distinguished myself), I certainly did—ahem—study a science called Logic, which my reckless companions——"

"A man," interrupted Herr Räumer, and addressing his remarks to me, "a man gets possession of a bundle of papers which contain facts the suppression of which is all-important. He may destroy them without fear; no one knows about them except a single person who has no other proof: he deliberately adopts a line of conduct towards that person—who is a hard man with no sentimentality about him, and who has never once forgiven anybody any single wrong, however small—which that person is bound to resent. And while he does this he hands back to that hard and revengeful person the very papers which alone give him the power of revenge. That is the most extraordinary line of action I have ever seen pursued, or ever read of. What am I to think of it? Is it part of a deeper plot?"

"Rubbish," said the Captain. "Can't a man avoid a dishonourable thing without having a plot? Do you suppose we are all schemers and conspirators?"

"The English are, indeed, a wonderful race,' said Herr Räumer.

"Can you not believe in a common act of honesty? Man—man!" said the Captain, "what sort of life has yours been?"

"I have seen a good deal of the world," Herr Räumer went on, meditatively. "I was in Vienna and in Paris in 1848. You got a considerable amount of treachery there. But I never before saw a case of a man who had ruin—yes—ruin staring him in the face—who was too honest to prevent it. Too honest."

He sat down and resumed his blue spectacles, and then took his hat, still holding the papers in his hands.

At last, he said, with an effort:

"I honour the first piece of genuine honesty that

I have ever, in the whole course of my life, actually witnessed. 'All men,' I said, at my leisure, 'are liars.' George Tyrrell, I give you back these papers. Take them and use them as you please. Best burn them. I give you the key of my safe; you can paint my name out to-morrow, if you please. Gentlemen, you will all three, I am sure, wish to keep this secret of our friend's life, as far as you know it, locked up and forgotten. Mr. Pontifex, you will say nothing about it to—to the she-dragon."

"I promised not to shake him, Johnny," Mr. Pontifex said, as if that engagement was sacred, and the only thing which prevented him from committing an act of violence.

"*Allons*," said the philosopher gaily, "let us be friends, Tyrrell; shake hands. I am going to leave this town, where I have spent ten years of my life, and shall return to-morrow or next day—to—to the Continent. I shall see you again, Ladislas. Perhaps this afternoon."

He stopped at the door.

"Tell Celia," he said, "that she is free, and that I shall always regret that I could not take her away with me."

He laughed and went away.

Then we all looked at each other as if we had been in a dream. There was actually a weak spot in the whole armour of cynicism with which Herr Räumer had clad himself, and we had found it.

Celia rescued. Andromeda free; the loathly dragon driven away; Andromeda's papa delivered from personal and private terror on his own account; and by the strangest chance, the whole brought about, though not continued, by me. I, who borrowed the key; I, who did a mean and treacherous thing, which gave the opportunity of an honourable and fearless action. After all, as Herr Räumer once said, the world would be but a dull place without its wickedness. It was as if Perseus, instead of flying through the air with winged feet and a sword swift to slay, conscious that the eyes of the Olympians were upon him, had crouched behind the rock when the Ægean wave lapped the white feet of the damsel, and from that safe retreat astonished the monster with a Whitehead torpedo. Nothing at all to be proud of. And yet no dragon assailed with a torpedo could be more astonished than our foreign friend at the exhibition of an un-doubted act of pluck and honesty. No doubt the admonitions of the Captain spurred on the hero, out of which I came, myself, as I felt, rather badly.

Let me say, once for all, that I do not know what the papers contained. Whether my old friend had committed a crime—whether it was forgery or burglary or anything else of which his conscience might have reproached him, and the opinion of the world looked askance upon, I do not know. Nothing more was ever said on the subject. The four actors in that little drama, including John Pontifex, maintained total silence. Even the safe disappeared. And neither then, nor at any subse-quent period, was the leading lawyer of the town, its Mayor, its most eminent Freemason, subjected to the slightest suspicion, attack, or misrepresenta-tion.

I asked to see Celia, but she had gone to her own room. I wrote a short note to her, sent it up, and went into the drawing-room, where Mrs. Pontifex and Mrs. Tyrrell, newly-reconciled, were sitting in great state and friendliness. Cake and

wine were on the table, not that the ladies wished
to sustain nature, but that their production, like the
pomegranate in the mysteries of Ceres, was a sym-
bolical act. It meant reconciliation, and Mrs.
Pontifex, who liked that the family should agree
in the way she thought fit, contemplated the glass
of sherry before her with an eye of peculiar satisfaction. I briefly narrated what had passed, gloss-
ing over the part that related to the papers, and
dwelling chiefly on Herr Räumer's disinterested
and generous conduct.

"And what were the threats!" asked Mrs.
Pontifex.

"There hardly appeared to be any threats," I
replied. "Herr Räumer made some allusion to
papers in the safe, but as he left papers and all with
Mr. Tyrrell, I presume they were unimportant, and
referred to private transactions."

"I must say, Clara," said Mrs. Pontifex, "that
George's behaviour was very good throughout. I
am much pleased. In a moment of weakness, no
doubt, he listened to the proposals of this foreigner,
who is, I admit, a clever and plausible person.
Both George and Celia said quite the right thing

in the right way, and I am greatly pleased. You say the man is gone, Ladislas?"

"Yes; he is going to leave the town, and return to the Continent."

"So much the better. He and his church on Sunday mornings, where he hoped to catch Celia! Fudge! I can forgive most things, Clara,"—she did not look as if there was much that she would forgive, but I am giving her own words—"hypocrisy I cannot forgive. I watched him once actually pretending to listen to one of John Pontifex's best sermons—that on Capernaum, which has, you remember, an application to the present condition of thoughtless mirth which has possessed our young people."

It was pleasant to feel that peace was restored between the two Houses of Pontifex and Tyrrell. More pleasant still to feel that a great danger had been averted.

Let me hasten with the story of this day big with fate. Imagine, if you please, the newly-born pride of Leonard as he introduced Celia to "My aunt, Miss Rutherford." Imagine the satisfaction and joy of that excellent lady on being quite certain that Moses—Moses with the spotty face and the passion for beer—was exchanged for this gallant and chivalrous young fellow—"he has got his father's graces," she whispered to me, "and his mother's sweetness."

Pass over the little tender scene where Miss Rutherford thanked the Captain solemnly for his care and bounty to "her boy,"—we cannot describe everything; there are some things which are better left unrecorded. It was a time of great joy. We had an early dinner at home—the Captain, as usual on great occasions, produced champagne. There were Celia and Miss Rutherford, both shy and a little frightened of each other, but hopeful that each would turn out as delightful as she looked. There was Leonard, of course, and the Captain, and myself. And be sure that Mrs. Jeram had not been forgotten, before dinner—else why those tearful eyes with which Miss Rutherford left our old housekeeper, and which spoke of talk over the poor creature who staggered three-and-twenty years before into Mrs. Jeram's arms, to die after giving birth to a man-child ? There was nothing

noisy or mirthful in our party—nothing to illus-
trate Aunt Jane's " present condition of thoughtless
mirth among young people." And but for the
disquiet of the morning deputation, I should have
been perfectly happy—as happy as Leonard and
Celia. And Leonard's face was like the sun in
June for beaminess and warmth.

We fell to talking over old times. The Captain
discoursed on the boys and their admirable qualities; Leonard told stories of Mrs. Jeram's *ménage*
and the fights he used to have with Moses; Miss
Rutherford listened with delight. She was in a
new atmosphere—this retired and secluded lady who
knew nothing of the world—the atmosphere of the
fighting world; the old Captain who had fought;
the young officer who had fought; I even belonged
to a fighting stock. And it was half-past two when
Celia took the elder lady away to introduce her to
her mother—and we began to clear the decks for
our deputation.

" You will let me be present," said the Captain.
" I have something to say to them. Rebellion,
indeed! What sort of a rebellion is that got
up by half-a-dozen exiles in foreign lands? No,

my boy, I don't deny the right of the Poles to rebel—but you shall not throw away your life till the whole nation rises. Then, if you like, you may go."

CHAPTER VIII.

THE DEPUTATION.

FIVE minutes for rest and reflection. What would this deputation of Poles say to me, and what was I to say to them? How to receive them? Was I to feign an ardour I did not possess; to put on the zeal of passionate Wassielewski, and clamour for the revenge which my English training made me hold to be impotent and barbaric; to throw in my lot with a knot of hopeless enthusiasts, and for the gratitude and respect I bore to one man to throw away my life in mad enterprise?

Or—the other line—was I to stand before them and say, like another Edgar Atheling—" I have no thought or care about the Fatherland; I am a Pole in name only ; I will not fight myself, nor lend you my name, nor join your ranks. Go your own way. 'Let the dead past be buried, and for the future the cause of Polish freedom shall have no aid from me." Or —lastly—could I say, " I am an Englishman, and not a Pole; I have an Englishman's sympathy with an oppressed people; but I see no sense in obscure risings, and I hate conspiracies ?"

And yet that was the truth. Wassielewski, a son of the soil, preserved all the prejudices and most of the ignorance of his country. His ideas of revenge were barbaric, but he did not know that; to shoot down Russians because twenty years before Russians had been made to commit unheard-of atrocities—as if we should suddenly resolve on murdering Hindoos in memory of Cawnpore—was in his mind a great, a noble, a patriotic act—more—an act which was pleasing in the eyes of his dead mistress, my mother, the Lady Claudia.

It is true that there were moments when the old conspirator's projects and plots had appeared to me admirable and worthy of emulation; when the thought of my father's cruel march through winter snows and summer heats on his weary way to be slowly done to death among the commonest

and vilest criminals maddened me; or when I
looked at the wooden cross he carved in the gloom
of the Siberian mine for me, his little child, whom
he was never to see again; or when I pictured him
as he had been seen a year or two before he died,
white-haired at thirty, aged and bent; or when I
remembered—the anguish of that memory has
never left me—the convoy of carts filled with children dragged from their mothers, the despairing
women who ran behind crying, shrieking, for their
little ones—my own poor mother among them.
Then, indeed, as now, I should be less than human
did not the blood boil in my veins; did not the
pulses quicken within me, did not a passionate desire for some kind of wild justice well up in my
heart. Revenge is unsatiable—had one killed with
the vigour of a Nero, the spilling of blood could
never quench the righteous wrath, or deaden the
pangs of sorrow and pain which would rise again
in thinking of that great suffering, that most terrible
crime. My mother, without doubt, has long since,
in the land where all tears are wiped away, forgiven.
I cannot forgive, for her sake. Perhaps I understand how sins against oneself may be forgiven, but

not sins against those we love. Lastly, against this conflict of opposing forces I had to place the calm good sense of the man whom most I had to consider —the Captain; the entreaties of the girl whom most I had to love; the firm decision of Leonard, that, happen what might, I should not be dragged into the plot.

I hope I have not tried to depict myself in any false colours. I was not a hero; in calm moments I saw the madness of the projected insurrection. I knew that such revenge as the old conspirator proposed was wild and useless; and yet, in his presence, by the enthusiasm of his ardour I was carried away so to speak, out of myself, and was ready to dare and to do. But since Leonard's arrival this infection of enthusiasm had been checked. By his help I saw things in their true light.

"You, Laddy?" said Leonard, laughing. "You to go out a-rebelling, with your face and your eyes? Go tell the Russians who and what you are; announce your intention of raising the standard of insurrection; they will laugh at you; they will take you in and make much of you, give you a piano, and refuse to let you come home again

because you play so well. We are no longer in
the days of the terrible Nicholas. Alexander has
begun a new era for Russia, which Wassielewski
and his friends cannot understand."

"I am too obscure," I said, bitterly, "even to do
any mischief."

"Any man," said the Captain, "can do mischief.
I was aboard a frigate once that was set on fire by
a powder-monkey. If you want to do mischief,
Laddy, in Poland or anywhere else, you can do
it."

I have mentioned once before little Dr. Roy, the
neatest and most dapper of tiny men. He, too,
must needs join in the general cry.

"I hear," he said, one day meeting me in the
street, "I hear a whisper that the Poles are stirring,
and they want to make use of you and your name."

I made no answer.

"Don't," he said impressively. "Believe a man
who once risked his neck in rebellion that it is a
most miserable line to take up. It was in Canada
—I dare say you have heard something about it.
We had grievances; we made a clamour about
them; the Government would not give in; so we

rose, and we did a little fighting. It wasn't very much, but it brought out pretty clearly all the miseries of revolt. We were put down. Everything that we rebelled to gain was granted by the British Government: everything, properly represented, would have been granted without rebellion. We had our revolt, our fighting, our loss of life; our destruction of property; our jealousies and personal squabbles; our treacheries and our treasons; our trials and our escapes—just all for nothing. No one got any good out of it at all, not even the half-dozen who went across to the States to gas about their bravery. Even the grandeur of being a rebel——" I thought of Herr Räumer's remarks on the rebel's enjoyment of being shot—"does not compensate for the trouble. And then to find out that you have no real grievances, after all. My own reward for the Canada rising was that I lost a capital practice in a very delightful Canadian town; that I was very nearly caught; that if they had caught me I should have been hanged; and that I am here on sufferance, because —which I am not afraid of—they might arrest and hang me to-morrow on the old account. For

Heaven's sake, Pulaski, keep out of rebellions. They won't give you back your father's lands."

All in the same tale; Herr Räumer's sneers and contempt were on the same side as Celia's prayers. Little Dr. Roy with his experiences was on the same side as the Captain.

And, against all these, I had to consider especially poor old Wassielewski. The old man, crazed with inextinguishable rage, looked on me as an instrument, ready to his hand, given him by Providence. For my part, I had to regard him as my saviour, the protector of my infancy, the faithful friend of my father, the devoted servant of my mother. Could I inflict upon him the cruel pain, the bitter humiliation, of seeing a Pulaski refuse to fight for Poland? Every Pole, he used to say, owed his life absolutely to his country. When he cannot fight to defend his rights, he ought to die in order that his people may not forget them.

I venture on a suggestion to rulers and despots. There are two or three ways of treating unsuccessful rebels. To shoot them publicly, transport them, torture their wives, and issue arbitrary laws of repression—all this is simply to give the Cause immortality. That is what the Russians have always done. The best way, surely, would be to forgive them, simply, and take away their arms, and to say, "My friends, you have now neither guns nor powder. We are not going to give you any. Sit down and grow your crops." Then such hot-headed irreconcilables as my old friend would be impossible. Or if they must be punished with death, then let it be done, as with Jugurtha and Catiline's conspirators, in the secrecy of some dark dungeon where newspaper correspondents cannot penetrate.

"Where are they, these heroes of Poland?" asked Leonard, laughing. He was determined that the thing should not be treated seriously. "Let us push the table back to the window—so. Now, Laddy, if you stand there on the hearthrug to receive them, it will be like holding a Levée. The Captain shall be your Court—I will be your *aide-de-camp*. And here they are."

Five men, headed by Wassielewski, came solemnly into the room, nearly filling it up. The last of the five shut the door carefully as if he was shutting out the world. But it opened again, and to my boundless astonishment admitted Herr Räumer, in his blue spectacles. He came in as if invited to take part in the ceremony, walked across the room, and stood in the window, his back to the light, beside the Captain. We formed two groups. I on the hearthrug, with Leonard at my right hand; and on the left the Captain, who contemplated the strangers with eyes of no favour, and beside him our German friend, to whom, since his magnanimous conduct in the matter of Celia, one felt an access of friendliness. And before us, the five men of my father's nation.

It was, as Leonard said, something like a Levée, only there was a certain incongruity about it which made one feel rather ashamed.

It was curious to consider that the men who stood before us were, so to speak, pledged to fall for their country. One thought of the prisoners brought out to fight their last battle with each other; every man resolute to make a brave show and please the thousands; every one hopeless of any escape; every one looking forward with a certain fearful expectation to the down-turning of the thumb; one or two, perhaps, the more aged men, not sorry to escape the miseries of captivity in the glorious rush and shout of vivid battle; some whose thoughts turned back——then Leonard touched my shoulder, and I gave my attention to things present. Wassielewski was there to introduce; not, he said, to speak. He wore a satisfied and even a glad expression. The long-wished-for moment had arrived. He had brushed his black coat and buttoned it tightly round his long lean figure; his white hair was combed back and fell behind his head, leaving his face standing out keen and eager with bright and deep-set eyes, and full white beard. His nervousness and restless manner was gone. You might think of him thus calm and collected charging his rifle for one more shot in a hailstorm from the advancing grey-coats.

The first of the four who came with him, and the most important, was a Pole about forty years of age; a tall, upright, and strong man, looking like a Frenchman in dress and the cut of his hair. His eyes had something of the wild look which characterised Wassielewski.

Wassielewski was about to introduce him to me,

when he broke away and advanced, speaking in French, with a certain gaiety of manner, and held out his hand—to Leonard.

"Count Pulaski," he said, "we are indeed rejoiced to find you like your father, among the friends of Poland. Wassielewski had not prepared us for such an accession to our ranks."

I was hardened by this time to any reference to my deformity, but I must own that it was not without a pang that I witnessed disappointment in his face, as Leonard bowed and indicated myself, the hunchback.

"Pardon, M. le Comte," he said. "This is my friend, Ladislas Pulaski."

The Pole's face fell, in spite of a polite attempt to disguise his disappointment. To be sure, there was some difference between a tall and handsome young man, whose very face commanded trust, and proclaimed him a natural leader, and myself, short, round-backed, and dreamy-eyed. We shook hands, and he said nothing, but stepped aside to make room for the other three. I received the greetings of all in turn. One of them was a short and thick-set man, apparently an artisan, a man of fifty or so, in ragged and threadbare blouse, whose face was decorated, like Wassielewski's, with a sabre cut. Another was a much older man in spectacles and black cloth clothes. This was a Professor in some American College, who had come across the Atlantic in vacation to see his compatriots, and learn the chances. The third was, I believe, an importation from Warsaw direct, who spoke nothing but Polish, and was pained to find that I could not understand him. It seems strange that Wassielewski should have allowed me to grow up in ignorance of so important a thing. As they stood before me I was struck with a resemblance which they all seemed to bear to each other. It was only for a moment, and was due, I suppose, to the Slavonic type of face. And oddly enough, Herr Räumer's face bore this same characteristic. I thought of Leonard's suspicions. Could he, too, be a Slav? But it was absurd to harbour suspicions against one who had actually been converted—that very morning—to the conviction that there may be honest men in the world.

"We are all friends of Poland, I suppose?" said the leader of the deputies, looking suspiciously

around. It was odd that no one, not even Wassielewski, took the least notice of Herr Räumer.

"I am an old friend of Ladislas," said Leonard.
"I am almost his brother, as Wassielewski knows.
But we will withdraw if you wish."

"He is an officer in the British army. He has
fought the Muscovite," said the old man. "He
may stay."

The first speaker, the Gallicised Pole, drew out
a paper.

"This is little more," he said, "than a meeting
to make the acquaintance of a young Pole of illustrious descent, great misfortunes, and undoubted
talents."

I bowed.

"Whose pursuits, we learn, have hitherto been
peaceful. We hear, however, with pleasure, that
we may confidently look for his adhesion whenever
we find it possible——"

"That is, immediately," said Wassielewski.

"To take practical steps in the desired direction."

"To call Poland once more to arms," explained
Wassielewski. "Speak, Ladislas Pulaski."

"Gentlemen," I said, speaking in French, "you

see me as I am ; deformed from my childhood, bearing a name which can never be made glorious by any achievement of my own. You know my story, and the fate of my father. Wassielewski has urged upon me to join you."

"And I," said Leonard, also in French, "have urged upon him the madness and folly of joining in your plans. Gentlemen—you, M. le Comte "— he addressed the chief of them—" are not all wild enthusiasts. If you concert any plan of rebellion, draw it up without consulting my friend, Ladislas Pulaski. He is not a soldier, nor is he of the stuff which makes soldiers. He is a poet and a musician. If you must pit the feeble resources of a province —I beg your pardon—a nation like Poland against the armies of a mighty empire which has been able to resist for two years the combined forces of England, France, and Turkey, do not add to your numbers a man who in the field will be useless to you, whose death can do you no good, and whose life may do others much good."

The leader hesitated. Then he whispered to Wassielewski.

And then the old Captain had his say.

"I do not," he said, stepping forward, and laying his hand upon my shoulder—"I do not unfortunately understand any language but my own. I have never regretted the fact till the present moment. Gentlemen, this boy is my son. I have adopted him, I have educated him, I refuse to let him go."

"The name of Poland—" began my old conspirator.

"In the name of Poland," said the Captain, "I would let him go if I thought he would be of any use. But this is not in the name of Poland. It is —pardon me if I am rough—in the name of a conspiracy. Assure me, if you can, that the nation is with you, and Ladislas shall go."

"No, no," cried poor old Wassielewski. "He comes of his own accord, he cannot be kept back, he fights for his mother's wrongs. Tell me, Ladislas, tell me, is not that the case?"

His voice trembled, his eyes were so pathetic that I could not resist their appeal. I took his hand, and pressed it, but I had no word to say.

The man they called the Count looked disappointed and uneasy.

"This is not," he said to Leonard, "quite the

reception which we expected. Still no doubt there is truth in what you urge, and besides—besides— nothing is quite certain. Be assured, M. le Capitaine," he addressed the Captain, "that we shall spare Count Pulaski if possible. If his name will help us, and if we can satisfy you that we obey the voice of the nation, we may call upon him——"

"If—if?" repeated Wassielewski. "Why, are the Poles gone mad to forget the glorious name of Pulaski?"

"Not mad, my friend," said the Count. "But twenty years have passed. In Polish villages, where there are no books and no papers, much is forgotten in twenty years."

I understood his look as he said these words. I was not to go. Of what use could I be, and who after all these years would be stirred for a moment by the intelligence that a Pulaski had joined the insurgents? Was my first feeling one of relief or of humiliation?

But the conference was brought to a sudden and unexpected end. The Count, looking round, perceived Herr Räumer standing modestly in the shade of the curtain.

"And who is this gentleman?" he asked. "Is he also a friend of yours, Count Pulaski?"

Before I could answer Herr Räumer replied for me. It was in his most mocking tone, which brought out the curious rasp in his voice. It was a voice which somehow haunted one—you could never forget it. I hear it still, sometimes, in dreams.

"A friend of Ladislas Pulaski, and a friend to Poland. Perhaps a closer friend than any of you. Pray proceed with your papers, M. le Comte."

It was the ragged workman, the man in the blue blouse, who sprang forward as if he had been shot, and pushing everybody aside, began gazing in the German's face, gesticulating and gasping.

"I know that voice," he cried. "I have heard that voice—many times. When? In Warsaw. From whom? From an agent of the police—the police—the Russian police!"

His voice rose to a shriek. Herr Räumer did not move or answer. His massive face seemed to be of marble as he stood there returning the other's gaze. And when the workman removed his blue spectacles he made no resistance, nor any sign.

"Who is this man, Wassielewski?" asked the Count.

"I do not know," he replied, carelessly. "I did not see him come in. I have seen him walking with Ladislas. He belongs to the town."

"Man!" cried the *ouvrier*, "do you not know his voice? Are you deaf then? Have you forgotten? Speak again—you. Speak, spy!"

But Herr Räumer did not speak. He folded his arms, looking down upon the little *ouvrier* with an expression of great contempt. But he did not speak.

The workman shrieked in a kind of rage.

"*Mais oui,*" he cried, "*mais oui.* I am not mistaken. Wassielewski, M. le Comte, look at this man, I say again. Look at him. Here is treachery, here is a spy of the Muscov. We are invited to meet a Pole—bah! a Pole who cannot speak his own tongue—and we find our enemy in the middle of us. *Mes frères,*" he looked round him with a face which revenge and hatred made a curious and hideous caricature, "*mes frères,* shall we let this man leave the house alive?"

"*Enfin,*" cried the Count. "Who is he? Is it any use, Count Pulaski, asking you who he is?"

"It is Herr Räumer," I said, "a German gentle-man, who has lived in the town for many years."

"Who brought him here?" asked the chief.

"He came in with you," I replied. "I thought Wassielewski brought him." The old man, puzzled and uneasy, shook his head. He was so eager to begin the fighting, this veteran rebel, that this pre-liminary · talk, even talk of traitors and spies, worried him. No: he had not brought in this stranger, he said.

Then Herr Räumer laughed and spoke.

"I came," he said, in that deep bass voice which jarred upon our nerves like a violoncello out of tune, "I came uninvited. Let that be understood. I was not asked to come by any one. I wished to make one in this gathering of Polish conspirators. It is a movement in which I take so deep an interest that I may be excused for wishing to know all that goes on."

Of course he was sneering, and, equally of course, he did not expect to be believed.

The Parisian Pole shrieked and danced with rage, ejaculating, cursing, pouring out imprecations with a volubility almost incredible.

"Here!" he cried, a little exhausted, "here! In the very presence of the young Count Pulaski. You, Wassielewski, look at him. Do you not know him?"

He lifted himself on his toes and hissed a name in Wassielewski's ear.

The old man staggered.

"Here—in the same town—all these years—and I not to know it"—he cried. "Not to know it——" Then he advanced upon Herr Räumer, tall, threatening, wild-eyed, waving his arms like the sails of a wind-mill.

"Oh! men—men—shall we kill him?"

He was hungry for the blood of the spy. Had he possessed a weapon, I think there would have been an end of him at once. Two of the others, the Professor and the Count, placed themselves before the door, and the man in the blouse danced round and round, loudly crying that he should be killed, and that at once.

"He is a spy—oh! Ladislas—hope of my heart —the son of my dear mistress whom this man murdered, what have you told him about us—about our plans?"

"Nothing, Wassielewski. Remember—I know nothing."

" He has told the spy nothing," Wassielewski repeated. "Have you eaten his bread, Ladislas? Have you entered his house ? Have you taken his hand ?"

"I have done all those things," I replied.

Herr Räumer laughed.

" He has done all those things. Why not, conspirator and rebel ?"

Wassielewski pointed to the man in the blouse.

" Tell him," he said, "tell Ladislas Pulaski why he should not have done those things."

" He should not have eaten his bread, or entered his house, or taken his hand, because the bread is paid for by Russia, because the house is the house of a Russian spy, and because the hand is red with Polish blood."

" And more—and more," said Wassielewski.

"Much more. That hand was the hand which arrested Roman Pulaski on his way to the Austrian frontier. It is the hand of the man who led the Cossacks when they robbed the Polish mothers of their children. Count Ladislas Pulaski, there stands the man who murdered your mother, and made you what you are."

" More," said Wassielewski. " More."

" It is the hand of the man who drove Roman Pulaski along the road from Warsaw to Siberia."

Leonard laid his hand upon my shoulder.

" Steady, Laddy—quiet, dear boy, patience."

Then the Count spoke.

" It is unfortunate. We might have known that Russian spies would be in this place somewhere. We did not expect to find one in our very midst."

" Among us all these years, and I never knew him," groaned poor Wassielewski. " Poles ! What shall we do to this man ?"

" Meantime said the Count, " we have to face the fact that he has been here to-day, that he knew of our coming, and the reason of it, and that all our proceedings will be reported immediately to St. Petersburg. This, at least, changes our plans."

" Not to-day's proceedings. For he shall die— he shall die !" cried the workman.

And then there was dead silence. The men looked at each other, as if asking who would strike the blow.

The Captain interfered.

"Gentlemen," he said, "do not forget that whatever this man is, or has been, he is in my house, and in England, and must be allowed to go unhurt. You cannot, as you might in Poland, kill him as a spy. That is impossible. You must let him go."

"Let him go?" cried the Parisian, springing to the front. "Never!"

I will do the man justice. He never flinched or showed the slightest fear. But the Count drew him back gently.

"Let him go in peace," he said. "In England we cannot shoot him. Go! all that we can do, Monsieur le Mouchard, is to parade your name, to describe your person, to make your calling impossible unless you can disguise yourself, and therefore to ruin you with the Secret Service Department. Go, loathed and accursed among men! Go, *canaille!*"

He turned from him with such a gesture as Peter might have made to Judas. Leonard, to my astonishment, took Herr Räumer by the arm, and led him to the door, going out with him, as the Poles fell

back right and left. Wassielewski and the man in
the blouse whispered together for a moment, and
then followed together. That boded ill for the spy,
and I was relieved, on the whole, to think that
Leonard was with him.

I was left alone with the three Poles and the
Captain.

" Count Pulaski," said the leader, " I greatly de-
plore this accident. I hoped that we should have
been able to lay before you all our plans to enlist
you in the cause, and to hold out hopes of an immediate insurrection."

" And now ?"

" Now, we have no plan. We must first find out
how far our secrets have been made known by that
man."

" Can I not help you ?" I asked. " I am—what
you see me—but I might do something yet for
Poland."

" You shall *live* for Poland," he went on, with a
sad but kindly smile. " No ; we shall not, as your
friend said, add murder to revolt in dragging you
away from your peaceful life. Think, if you can,
sometimes, of those who have personal sufferings

and degradations burning in their souls. You have none. My back has felt the Russian stick; my cheek yet burns with the Russian blow. Still, you have the memory of your father's death, and you cannot love the Russian cause. Forget us as soon as you can. I shall take Wassielewski away, and leave you free. We shall have meetings, I suppose, but you will not be asked to join. Everything is uncertain, because in London, Paris, everywhere, the *mouchards* throng. And, of all *mouchards*, the most crafty, the most difficult to detect, is the Russian. I wish you farewell, Count Pulaski."

He took my hand and was gone, followed by his three friends, and I was left alone.

This was the end of my grand deputation.

I was free; my promise would never be fulfilled; I was relieved of my pledge. And I was profoundly humiliated. For I was allowed to go as one who could be of no use to the cause. I saw the disappointment on the chief's face when he turned from Leonard to me; I saw the readiness with which he acquiesced in Leonard's expostulation; I was of no use to him or to his party. The last of my race was another Edgar Atheling.

And would they think—no—they could not—that I had revealed the plot to this Russo-German spy? Or that I was a foolish creature who could not hold his tongue?

CHAPTER IX.

HERR RÄUMER'S INTENTIONS.

IN the street Leonard released his hold of Herr Räumer's arm.

"You are free," he said. "Go your own way."

The spy laughed.

"Of course I knew there was no danger. The danger begins now. Come with me to my lodgings. I have something to say to you."

Leonard followed him.

In his own place the man opened a bottle of hock, and after offering a glass to Leonard, who refused, drank glass after glass without stopping.

"Nothing," he said, "steadies the nerves like hock. So you will not drink with a member of the Russian Secret Service? No. You will not sit down in his room? No. You will not take his hand? No. You think it a disgrace to belong to that service? Good. That is not a disgrace, but it is disgraceful to be found out, and I do not disguise from you that it will not do me good at headquarters to have been discovered. After all, they will remember that I have had a good long run.

"Our friend in the blue blouse"—he sat down and crossed his legs—"was quite right, though he put things roughly. The Poles *cannot* see the other side of the question. That is why I wanted to explain to you one or two little things."

He paused, as if trying to find words.

"I cannot hope," he said, "to make you understand that the execution of orders in the Police is no more disgraceful than in the Army. I did arrest Roman Pulaski. I tracked him down, and caught him just upon the frontier. That was my duty. I did escort him part of the way to Siberia, whither he walked on foot. That was my duty. The sentence was the Czar's. I was his servant. Do you blame me? No; you cannot. As regards the other charge about the children, that is also partly true. I was not in charge of the carts, but I rode part of the way with them. I am in no mood for lying, or for defending myself with you, but I ask you to let young Pulaski know that this is the first I have heard about his connection with that day. I did not know, when I first made his acquaintance, that he was one of the victims of that—that—excess of zeal on the part of our Cossack friends. I knew nothing about his mother. You may believe me or not when I tell you that when I made his acquaintance—when I found him to be a poet and a dreamer—I resolved to prevent him if possible from being led to death by a madman. Do you blame me for that?"

"Yes," Leonard replied. "I blame you for ever speaking to him or knowing him. I blame you—because you are a spy."

"A servant in the Secret Service Department. Yes, and in that capacity I have been of use to my country."

"I dare say you have," said Leonard. "I do not care to hear about that. I have only one more thing to say. Did you happen, when you came away, to catch the expression in old Wassielewski's eyes?"

"I did. I watched all the eyes. Shall I tell you what they said as plainly as eyes can speak? That boy looked at me with a sort of wonder, as if it was not possible; the Professor with curiosity; the Count with disappointment, but no surprise. I know the Count, he is a clever man, and, if he does not get shot in Poland, will rise in Paris. The old Captain would have liked to hang me up at the yardarm, and the other two, Wassielewski and our Parisian, looked murder."

"I came with you, to warn you."

"Thank you very much; I need no warning."

"What are you going to do?"

"Murder and revenge," he repeated. "That sounds ugly. But I have seen the look of murder in a good many eyes before now. The look does not kill. I shall do nothing."

"You will remain here?"

"Yes, here—in this town—in this house. They may come up here to murder me. I have pistols. I sleep with the door locked. I shall not be frightened away by any pair of Polish patriots."

"That will not do at all," said Leonard. "You must go away."

" Must ? and why ?"

He explained that there were other reasons besides the fear of those two. These Poles would spread it abroad that he was a Russian spy ; the town was full of sailors only a year or so from the Crimean War, and that an English mob were generally rough.

Lastly, Leonard assured him that so far as lay in his power he should take care that he should enter no respectable person's house, that his profession should be told everybody, and that a highly coloured description of the deputation scene should be forwarded to the local and to the London papers.

Then Herr Räumer gave way.

" You are a pertinacious man," he said, " and you want to see me go. Well. I will go to-day. Will that satisfy you ?"

" I want, for the sake of poor old Wassielewski, to avoid a scandal. " See,"—Leonard pointed to the window—" the little man in the blouse is watching you in the street."

This was indeed the case. He was marching backwards and forwards, gesticulating and inces-

Herr Räumer's Intentions.   151

santly casting an eye at the door of the enemy's house.

"Go in the daytime," said Leonard. "There is a train to London at five—go by that."

"Perhaps," said the spy. "Perhaps by a later train. But I shall go to-day. That I promise you, for Wassielewski's sake."

"All this," he went on, after more hock, "all this, I confess, is horribly annoying to me. I had formed a pleasant plan for the future which has been entirely disarranged. At sixty-two one does not like to have one's plans upset. I pictured to myself ten years of ease and retirement from active work, giving my advice and experience to the Department, going on those special missions reserved for the higher officers of the service, decorated, pensioned, and living at St. Petersburg with a young and beautiful wife. I confess I am disappointed. Now, I dare say, I shall never marry at all. After all, he who expects nothing from life gets the most. I am content."

"I came away after that," said Leonard. "What a man it is! He has no shame, he glories in his trade. I hope he will go, as he promised, but I am not easy about it. I should like to watch old Wassielewski, or lock him up. And it seems too much to think that he will go away in broad daylight like a man who isn't a spy. Most likely he will steal away in the dark by cross-cuts and lanes, and on tiptoe, after the manner of a stage spy."

CHAPTER X.

A FAMILY GATHERING.

So all seemed settled, and there was nothing at all left for us but to rejoice and be glad together. All is well that ends well. Leonard and Celia were to be married, the Captain and I were to go on together as of old, there was to be no more threatening of insurrections, life would resume the same calm which is so dull to look back upon, and yet so happy while it lasts. We celebrated the event of Celia's engagement immediately by a family gathering that evening at Mr. Tyrrell's. It was also an entertainment in commemoration of the reconciliation of Aunt Jane with her niece, and, if on that account alone, the best tea things were produced, and there was a lavish expenditure in the matter of muffins and tea-cakes.

Nothing shows the march of civilisation more than the decay in the consumption of muffins and tea-cakes. Nobody has tea at all now, except at five o'clock, because those who remember what a tea-party used to be cannot call handing tea round in trays having tea. Nobody sits down now to a table covered with cake in various forms, but it was in those days the commonest form of entertainment. I suppose everybody of the middle classes looked upon a tea-party as the chief instrument of social intercourse, and Mrs. Tyrrell was by no means singular in attaching a symbolic importance to her best tea-service.

Nothing could have been finer than the manner of Aunt Jane. She kept Celia beside her. She offered no objection whatever when her husband, presuming on the unusually fine weather, ventured to ask for more sugar. She made no allusion to any Christian privileges, either by way of example or admonition, and having found out that Miss Rutherford's father had been a distinguished writer and preacher of the same school as herself, that is, of the severest Calvinistic type, she received her with marked cordiality. Calvinism in that gentle lady, however, was so tempered with native kindness that it lost all its terrors.

As for Mr. Tyrrell, the removal of the weight upon him almost restored him to his youth. He made jokes, he laughed; he was attentive to his wife, he was not only happy again, but he had recovered his old confidence and importance.

In the evening we played, Celia and I, then we sang duets, then Celia sang by herself, but only one song, because everybody wanted a little confidential talk with her in turn.

First it was Aunt Jane.

"Well, my dear," she said, with an inclination of the head in the direction of Leonard, "as you have made your choice I suppose there is nothing more to say."

"But, dear Aunt"—well-brought-up young people in those days did not venture on such a respectful endearment as "Auntie"—I should like to have seen any one address Mrs. Pontifex as "Auntie"—"you have no objection to Leonard, have you?"

"No—no," she replied critically. "He is, I am

told, though not yet a Professing Believer, not without hopes. A husband, my dear, is what a wife makes him. You would hardly believe, perhaps, the trouble which my husband, John Pontifex, has given me by the violence of his natural inclinations. All men, in the matter of eating and drinking, require strong and constant discipline. That you will have to administer with constant searchings into your own conscience. Mere worldliness I need hardly warn you against. You must not encourage your husband's tendency to over-estimate the value of earthly distinctions, though I am glad to learn from his aunt that he comes of a County Family. We who have been blessed, by Providence, with County connections would be blind to our privileges did we not remember that fact. You will never forget your own maternal connections. I refer rather to military distinction. And, above all, my dear, guard against inordinate affection. I need hardly warn you that before marriage any demonstration of—of—of what I suppose you call Love, is highly improper. No girl who values herself, or calls herself a Christian gentlewoman, would allow her lover to kiss her on the lips. My first husband, it is true, once surprised me by kissing what he called my marble brow. I never allowed John Pontifex more than the tip of my fingers. After marriage you will find they are not so anxious for kissing. Remember that, my dear.

"He is what the world calls handsome, I fear," —as if it were a blot upon his moral character— "and he has been successful so far." Here she sighed, as if that was another moral blot. "But he is young. I could have wished you to remain, as I did, single to the age of thirty, or even forty; you then might have chosen a man some years your junior, and enjoyed the privileges which age and maturity add to marriage. That has been the case with John Pontifex."

Then it was the Captain.

"Come to me, Cis, my pretty," the old man called her to sit beside him. "Come and tell me all about it. And so you have accepted my boy Leonard, have you? Happy man! I believe I am jealous of him. You must not forget the old house by the Milldam."

"No," said Cis. "I shall not forget the old house, or its owner."

"When is Leonard going to take you away? Don't let him hurry you, Celia. We shall be dull when you are gone."

They protested to each other like a pair of lovers, the old Captain and the girl. I believe she loved the old man as well as any one, after Leonard.

She looked shyly happy, and was as radiant as a moss-rose half blown with the sunshine on it. Her eyes kept lifting to Leonard as if she could not bear that he should be out of her sight for a moment, and they were full of a new, strange, and wonderful light. A change had fallen upon her all in a day. A man loved her, and she could give him love for love. It was no mushroom passion, the growth of a ballroom, brought into being by a pair of bright eyes, an intoxicating waltz, the whirl of white arms, and the glamour of music; it was a life-long affection, suddenly ripened into love by the touch and words of Leonard the magician. I have watched other maidens since then, and have seen that look in some of their eyes, but not in all. " She loves him ; loves him not," I say, according to the light of her eyes.

"And not a word for me, Cis, for my own private ear?"

"What shall I say, Laddy?"

"Are you perfectly content and happy, my dear?"

"Yes, Laddy, quite, quite happy. There is nothing that Heaven can give me more. I am more happy than I can say. And you? There is no more danger about this Polish business?"

"Happily, none; I am free. My poor old Wassielewski exaggerated the certainty of his insurrection. He saw what he wished to see. The Poles are not ready yet, and, so far as I am concerned, they would not have me if I wanted to go. Of that I am certain."

"I am glad. I could not bear to think of you breathing revenge and bloodshed. You will stay at home and make the world happier with music, Laddy. You must be a great composer."

And then Mr. Pontifex claimed her.

"I have, I believe," he began, "to offer my—ahem—my congratulations on so auspicious an event as your—in fact—your engagement. Marriage is an honourable condition, although not, as the

Papists ignorantly make it, one of the Sacraments of the Church. We have known the young man your—your—in fact, your betrothed—for many years, and we rejoice to find that he has not only distinguished himself as greatly in—ahem—in action—as others," meaning himself—"sometimes distinguish themselves at Oxford in examination, but he has also been enabled under Providence to recover what some would consider an indispensable condition of acceptance with a family of respectability—I mean respectable connections of his own."

Celia laughed.

"At all events, we liked Leonard before he had found Miss Rutherford."

"That is most true. You will, however, Celia, be rejoiced to learn that Miss Rutherford herself belongs to a County family, and that Leonard, both on his father's side and his mother's, is of an excellent stock."

"I am glad if Leonard is glad."

"Your Aunt—in fact, Mrs. Pontifex—thinks that steps should be taken to put Leonard in communication with his father's family, a subject on which she proposes to speak at another occasion. For the present, Celia, my dear, she will probably do no more than invite you to dinner. Mrs. Pontifex has resolved, I may say, upon having a dinner. I do not myself, I confess greatly admire our own, or rather her style—ahem—of entertainment. I have, on one or two such occasions, arisen from the meal with an unsatisfied appetite. But we think too much on carnal things."

And all the time Leonard was talking with his newly-found Aunt. It seems a prosaic ending for one who never had a father. Leonard was a foundling, or next door to it, he attained to the three-and-twenty without knowing where he came from, and he then, having just occasion to thank Heaven that his father was no more, found—an Aunt. No lordly lineage, no rich and childless father brooding over the irretrievable past, no accession to wealth and fortune, only a widow Aunt, with a small income, only a confirmation of the fact stated by the poor dying mother that he was a gentleman by birth. Yet the confirmation pleased Leonard as much as if he had been proved an earl by birth, and

was declared the missing heir to boundless acres
and a genealogy going beyond Noah.

It was a quiet evening, with no general conversation, but always these sub-divisions and sections
of two and three. It was not late when we
separated, and Leonard, leaving Miss Rutherford
to the care of Cis, came with the Captain and
myself.

The Captain had his pipe and glass of grog, and
went upstairs, to turn in. We, left alone, sat silent,
looking into space, at the open window, wrapped in
our thoughts.

Surely, I considered, Leonard is the spoiled child,
whom nothing can spoil, of Fortune. He has fought
his way through the briars and brambles of poverty
and obscurity, the friendly hand of Fate warding
off bullets, bayonets, and the breath of disease. He
has come back to us, bearing the Queen's Commission, a successful hero, where so many equally
heroic, only less successful, had fallen by the way,
and now lie dead on the plains of India or in the
Cemeteries of Scutari and the Crimea—he had the
gift of Good Luck—*la main heureuse.* Whatever
he tries to do, he does well. To be sure, he does it

with all his might. What we call Luck, a small and degraded word, the ancients called Fate, because to them success and failure meant much more than they mean now. To lose your high estate; to be a slave who once was Queen of Troy with gallant sons foremost in the fight—that was Fate. To return in triumph, leading the captive Kings at the chariot-wheel—or to be one of the captive kings, shorn of all your former magnificence —Louis Quatorze with the wig off—that was Fate.

To sit in obscurity, to go on living upon a small income, to be unknown, when you know yourself as good a man as he whose name is in every paper, whose voice is heard at every gateway, whom the Lord Mayor delighteth to honour—that is Luck. It seems at first to be a thing quite independent of personal virtues, except that you ought not to be conspicuously vicious ; Luck was with Leonard. And yet he was conspicuously, like all successful men one who deserved his Luck.

" What are you thinking of, Laddy ?"

" I am thinking that of all men on earth you are at this moment the happiest."

"I think I am, indeed," he said, softly. "I have Celia ; I have my Commission and my medals ; and now I am no longer a waif and stray in the world, come from nobody knows where, but I have my place with the rest, and can talk of my forefathers like any Howard."

CHAPTER XI.

THE POLE'S VENGEANCE.

IT was past eleven o'clock, but the day had been exciting, and we could not think of sleep. It was a hot night, too, with a little wind, but a full bright moon shining in the placid waters of the Milldam. The town was very quiet ; in the kitchen, a cricket chirped loudly ; in a neighbouring garden was baying a foolish dog, driven nervous by the moonlight which, as everybody knows, makes wandering spectres, if there are any about, visible to dogs. Frightened at length by the sound of his own voice, perhaps awed by a more than commonly dreadful ghost, he left off barking and retreated to his kennel. Then we were quite quiet, and sat face to face in silence.

My nerves that night were strung to the point at which whatever happens brings relief. I felt as if something was going to happen.

So did Leonard.

"Come," he said, "we must either talk or go off to bed. I feel as if something oppressive was in the air. Is it thunder? No; it is a clear and beautiful night. Let us go into the garden."

We went to the end of the garden, and stood on the stone coping, looking over the broad sheet of water.

"You are content, Laddy, with the turn things took this afternoon?"

"Yes," I said, "content and yet humiliated. Why did I ever learn the story of my people?"

"Poland has no claim upon you," said Leonard. "Your education — your disposition — everything makes you a man of peace. Stay at home and make the name of Pulaski glorious in art."

"Who is that, Leonard? Listen."

An uneven step in the quiet street. That was nothing, but the step seemed familiar. And it stopped at our door. And then there was rapping, a low rapping, as if the late caller wanted to come in confidentially.

There was a light burning in the hall, and Leonard snatching it up, opened the door.

It was Wassielewski. And then I knew, without being told, that some dreadful thing had happened.

"Let me come in," he said. "I have a thing to say. Are you two alone?"

"Alone," echoed Leonard. "Come in."

"The soldier," murmured the old Pole. "Good; he will understand."

As he stood in the light of the candles, I was conscious of a curious change that had fallen upon him. His eyes had lost their wild and hungry brilliancy; they were soft and gentle; but his cheeks were flushed, and though he held himself upright, his hands trembled.

"I am here to tell you, Ladislas Pulaski, that you are avenged upon the murderer of your mother."

"Wassielewski! You have killed him!"

I knew it without another word from him. The spy was dead, and the hand of my poor old friend was red with his blood.

"Yes. I have killed him," he said, gently.

"Tell us all," said Leonard. "Courage, Laddy, courage. And speak low."

"It was in fair fight," said Wassielewski. "I am no murderer. Do not think that I murdered him. We watched him, that good and true man from Paris and I, all day. We knew that he would escape by train if he could, and so we drew lots. One was to go to the station and watch there. He was to take a ticket for the same station as the spy, he was to telegraph for friends to meet him in London, he was to get out with him, he was to follow him, and he was to find out where he went. Because, you see, we meant that this man should do no more mischief to Poland. The other one was to watch the house, and follow the spy whenever he came out.

"The lot fell to me to watch the house. The other man went to the railway station. But the spy will send no more intelligence to St. Petersburg. He lies dead in a meadow beneath the town walls. I killed him there."

He spoke quite calmly, and as if he was merely stating a fact which we had every reason to expect.

There was, however, no trace of bravado in his tone.

"I watched outside, from a window in a house opposite where they know me, from four o'clock till ten. Six hours. But I was not impatient, because I knew that the Lord had delivered him into my hands. After I thought things over, I perceived clearly that it was I, and not you, Ladislas, who was to avenge your mother. So I waited with patience, and, as one must guard against every accident, I even ate and drank.

"It is light, now, till nine, and there is light enough to see across the street till past ten. Soon after sunset I saw that he had lit a lamp, and was destroying papers. When he had gone through all the papers, he began to pack a trunk. I saw him put up his clothes; I saw him write an address on a card; and then—a quarter before ten was striking from St. John's Church—he took that long cloak of his which you know, and put out the gas. There is a night train at half-past ten. He was going to take it, and to send for his boxes afterwards. So I went out after him.

"When he saw me, which he did at once, because

he turned at the sound of footsteps, he stopped and waited for me. 'You propose murdering me,' he said. I told him that he was quite mistaken, and that, if he had used his opportunities of knowing the Poles better, he would understand that Poles never murder people at all—having contracted a horror of murder from the contemplation of such murders as those of Roman and Claudia Pulaski.

"'What do you want with me, then?' he asked.

"'I want to fight you,' I said. 'I intend to fight you.'

"He laughed at first, and asked me if I thought him such a fool as to fight with a mad Polish exile —he, a Russian official.

"Then I told him that he should not escape a duel; that if he were to call the police, it would be of no use, because others were waiting for him, that if he escaped the town, the telegraph had sent messages to London, and he would meet with the Poles on arriving there; and if he tried to fly anywhere else, he would be watched, traced, and made to fight then.

"'Madman,' he said, 'what are we to fight with?'

"Then I showed him two long knives, which I have had for years, never thinking what a use I should put them to. Knives like short swords, only without the hilt. And I told him he should have his choice. But fight he must.

"He hesitated, considering. He saw very well that what I offered him was his best chance. Man for man. If he killed me, he would probably get away somehow. My comrade was at the station, and might be eluded. Then he was younger and stronger than I.

"'You understand,' I said, 'the duel is to be *à outrance*. I shall kill you, unless you kill me first.'

"'Where are we to fight, madman ?' he asked.

"I told him of a place I knew of, a meadow surrounded with trees, beneath the town wall. He knew it, too, and nodded.

"'You are younger,' I said. 'You have that advantage; on the other hand, you have a bad cause, and I a good one. You will fight your best, but you have to fight two, not one—Roman Pulaski as well as Wassielewski. One is dead, and it is hard to fight a dead man.' He laughed ; he was no coward, that man. No, no; I never said that the Muscovites are cowards; but it is not well to laugh at dead men. The dead arm may still strike. He was no coward; he was brave, like all his countrymen. But he laughed at the dead; he said he was ready to fight a dozen dead Poles. 'But as for you, mad old patriot and fool, I will not fight you. Stand out of my path.' 'Do you wish to fight in the street?' I asked him. 'Here is your knife; here is mine. For fight you shall.' I suppose he saw that it was of no use to refuse, for he took the knife and cursed me. He could curse very well, that man. I said nothing, because the Lord had delivered him into my hand, and it is not good to begin a fight with cursing. So I walked beside him, feeling the point of my knife— at his left hand, because the Muscovite spies are treacherous, and he might have tried to stab me had I been on the other side. One has to be careful with such men as that."

"I think, Wassielewski," said Leonard, "that you had better sit down and rest. This talk is too much for you."

The old man was swaying backwards and forwards, flinging about his arms, acting the scene, imitating his enemy's voice and gestures, so that one could picture the big, ponderous-looking spy staring straight in the Pole's face in his insolent, cynical, and contemptuous way. But his voice grew shaky, and his lips were parched.

·Leonard poured out a glass of spirits and water, which he drank greedily.

"Aha!" he cried, "I forgot that I was thirsty. Now I can go on."

"Laddy," said Leonard, "don't stare at him with that scared face. Courage, dear boy. Wait till we come to the end. Keep your imagination quiet now, above all times. If you are ready, Wassielewski, to go on——"

"Yes, I am ready. Oh! yes. Quite ready.

"It is a beautiful moonlight night. Almost like a moonlight night in Poland. I thought of the night marches we used to have in 1833, singing as we went through the woods—those were the times ·for the Poles, when we met the enemy in the morning, and cut him off before he was awake. And then I thought of the moonlight nights—ah! how many years ago—fifty years and more, when

Napoleon promised to free Poland, and all of us flocked to his army—and the merry days when we danced all night long with the Polish girls, long before the Muscovite forbade them to wear their own dress, and stopped their dancing altogether. The more I thought of these things, the more happy I felt to be walking side by side with the spy. Because I knew, oh! yes, I knew very well indeed, that I was going to kill him.

"And as I was back in Poland I thought of other things. It is a good thing that one can think so quickly. I was with the rebels again. I had in my hands the very gun which the Lady Claudia gave me. I was creeping in the underwood towards a Russian outpost; I was sentinel all night in the insurgents' camp; I was fighting behind a barricade; I was following Roman Pulaski in a charge; I was running after the carts in which the children were being carried away; I was crying over the dead body of Claudia with little Ladislas in my arms—I saw it all—all my past life, as well as I see you, Ladislas, and you, Leonard Copleston, before me at this minute. It was a sign to me that I was to gain some signal and great honour.

And no honour could be so great to me as the killing of that spy. Because I knew very well indeed that I was certain to kill him.

" Then a strange thing happened. I saw that on the other side of the spy, marching silently, was your dead father, Roman Pulaski. His face was stern and hard, not like the happy face he wore when he married his wife, when he tossed his child, and when he set off to fight the Russians, but stern and hard. He meant that justice should be done. There was the memory of his long march to Siberia in his look, and the years of misery in the mine. He was worn and haggard, and his hair was grey, though his step was firm. Roman Pulaski was going to fight for me. It seemed unfair for the man between us, but it was justice.

"At my right was Lady Claudia. She took no notice of the spy who was going to be killed, not the least notice, because he was beneath her contempt. But she whispered in my ears gracious words, ' Faithful Wassielewski ; brave old servant ; this one battle over, and your work is done. Courage and patience. You shall see me again before long, when this man is killed.'

"We marched in silence, we four, with the steps of two, side by side along the deserted streets. No one met us, the patrols were all gone back to their barracks, and no policeman passed us. It would have astonished a policeman to see four persons walking together, and two of them dead. When we got to the place where we were to fight—you know it well, Ladislas. It is where you and the lady walk sometimes, and sit among the flowers— we got over the gate side by side, and walked across the grass."

Good Heavens! The man, then, was lying dead among the buttercups in our own meadow under Celia's Arbour, the place where we had talked, played, and sauntered so many, many times so many years.

"He said nothing, but kept his eyes on me—he did not seem to take any notice of Roman Pulaski —while he threw off his cloak and hat. It is a full moon, and the meadow was as light almost as day. He chose his own position, where the moon- shine fell full upon my face, so that it might blind my eyes. Fool! As if it mattered while Roman Pulaski was by my side. I laughed at his madness, and took the place he left for me. The Lady Claudia remained behind. It was not for her to watch the fight. She stood beneath the trees where I saw her white robes fluttering in the breeze. You cannot expect a saint in Heaven to look at the punishment of a spy.

"Foot to foot, and in each right hand a knife. He fought well, he sprang upon me like a lion, he struck at me here, there, everywhere, but he struck at me in vain, because all his blows were warded off. He was a brave man, but he fought against the dead. All the time he cursed and swore at me for a madman, a mad old Pole, a mad old lunatic, everything that was mad. But I never answered watching his knife, and waiting my chance. And close beside me stood Roman Pulaski, tall and strong as in life, but his face was hard and stern.

"And then the chance came, and he fell. My knife was plunged to the handle in his heart. I had no scratch upon me, no hurt or wound of any kind. And when he fell I thought of Lady Claudia's words, ' Only this one battle left, and your work is done.' I am past seventy years of age. I fear I shall kill no more spies.

I looked at him as he lay on the grass. There was a pool of blood, the knife was in his heart, and he was quite dead. And then I came away.

"Before me strode Roman Pulaski, and presently he joined the Lady Claudia. She waved her hand to me, and they both went out of sight hand in hand.

"Then I thought I would come here and tell you, Ladislas, that your enemy is dead. He can do you no more harm and Poland no more harm. The Czar has one spy the less."

He ended his story, which he told throughout with a quiet and suppressed vehemence, and with the exultation of one who has done a noble and a brilliant action. Much brooding and a solitary life had driven him mad. He could see no cause for regret or repentance, he had slain his enemy in fair fight, he was the instrument of Providential retribution, he obeyed the behests of his dead mistress, and he had no doubt whatever that the phantoms of his disordered brain were real visitants from the realms of the upper world.

Real visitants! They were real to me while I listened with trembling lips to his story. I felt the great horror which, as they tell, falls always upon those who see, or think that they see, the spirits of the dead. It was as if in the room with Wassielewski were those sacred Shades whom I longed but dreaded to look upon. And for the moment the horror of the murder, the image of the dead man lying on his back in the long grass, were lost in the eagerness of that desire that they would show themselves to me as they showed themselves to their old servant, and speak to me as they spoke to him. They never came, they never spoke, no voice or whisper from the grave has come to me, nor will come. And yet I doubt not that some time I shall see them both in earthly beauty glorified, and with earthly love transformed into heavenly love.

"That will be best. She said my work was done. In Poland I shall find a grave near hers. I know where she lies beside the road, because I buried her. I will seek out the spot and die there too. My work is done."

Leonard listened gravely. He had not interrupted him, except to ask for the knife. Now he looked at me with a pitying despair on his face.

He could do nothing.   The poor old man would be tried for murder.   And he was quite mad.

Meantime Wassielewski sat down and rested. The exaltation was dying out in his brain, and he looked wearied.

And as we asked each other in despairing looks, Leonard and I, what to do next, we were startled by a step outside.

"Good Heavens!" I cried.   "Who is that?"

Wassielewski had left the door open.   The steps came into the hall; then we heard the street door closed gently.   And then our own door opened slowly, and a muffled voice, hoarse and thick, whispered through the opening:

" All friends here?"

CHAPTER XII.

AN UNEXPECTED FRIEND.

" ALL friends here ?"

Leonard sprang to the door and threw it open. In the doorway stood—good Heavens! was it Herr Räumer himself, wrapped in his long cloak, a military cloak which fell to his heels, and was thrown over his left shoulder ?—a figure the same height as the spy, and having a black felt hat pulled forward over his face.

"The spy's cloak," said Wassielewski quietly, and without the least symptom of alarm or discomposure, "and his hat. But I killed him."

The figure cautiously removed the hat.

That action disclosed a head covered with short, thick, and stubbly red hair, a face whose expression was one of cunning, impudence, and anxiety all combined : such a face as you may meet on the tramp along country roads, one that glances upwards at you as you pass the owner supine in the shade, or that you may see sitting outside a village beer-shop, or where the more adventurous class of tramps, vagrants, and gipsies most resort. Not the thin hatchet face with receding forehead and protruding lips which belongs to the lowest class of London habitual criminals, the face of a class whose children will be *crétins*, the face which is the result of many generations of neglect, overcrowding, and vice. This was the face of a strong and healthy man, and yet the face of a sturdy rogue. And in removing the hat, the fellow looked round with assurance and nodded cheerfully to Wassielewski.

" His cloak," said Wassielewski, pointing to the garment, " and his hat. But it was I who killed him."

" Right you are, guv'nor," responded our new visitor cheerfully. " His cloak it is. Likewise, his hat it is. And I see you a-killing of him. But don't you be frightened, mate. All friends here ?"

He turned his impudent face to us, as if we were a pair of accomplices.

"About the putting of that chap," he jerked his finger over his shoulder, "out of the way—I don't want to say nothink disagreeable. There's lots as ought to be put out o' the way, only there's the scraggin' after it—an' I do hope, guv'nor, as you won't be scragged. Bless you, there's a many gets off, on'y the papers don't say nothink about it. And don't you frighten yourselves, young gents both. I've got a word to say as'll please all parties, give me time to say it. Lord help you, I feel like a pal a'ready to this old guv'nor here—and do you think I'd split upon a pal? Gar!"—he made a gesture indicative of contempt for those who split on pals —"and if you could oblige me with a drop o' some-think to drink an' a bite of supper, and p'r'aps a mouthful o' baccy, I could say that word in a more friendly way. Lord! let's all be friends."

He sat down at the table, and, throwing off the cloak, disclosed the uniform of a convict.

"Things are getting mighty pleasant," said Leonard. "Pray, are there any more of you outside? Who is going to turn up next?"

"No one, noble Cap'en. No one—I'm by myself, and I wish to remain as such. There ain't no more of us—and we don't want no more. As you see, a convict I am and a convict I've been for the best part of a twelvemonth, working in that blamed Dockyard of yours. Is that rum in the decanter?" —the Captain's spirit-case, in fact, stood on the sideboard, with a ham placed there for his supper, and not removed. "Give me a drop, my noble Cap'en, I haven't tasted rum for—not too much water—Lord! it's delicious," he gasped, as he drank off half a tumblerful, which Leonard gave him. "Another glass? And is that ham? I've really got somethink important to tell—jest a morsel of that ham. There's no ham to be got in quod. Ham —*and* rum—Moses! what a chance!"

We gave him the ham and a plate, and contained our impatience while he sat down and made a supper. He devoured hurriedly, and yet took a long time, because he devoured an immense quantity. Either Nature had gifted him with a profound appetite, or the diet of the hulks was meagre. In either case, I never saw a man put away such an enormous quantity of provisions at one time. He wolfed the meat as if he had never tasted meat before, and drank as much rum and water as Leonard would give him. It was like a horrible nightmare to see that man calmly devouring his food while we waited his completion of his meal, as if a homicide was a matter that could wait to be talked about till things of greater importance, such as supper, were first discussed. But his appearance served one cause. It helped to calm one's nerves after the first shock of Wassielewski's story. The old man sat silent and steady, looking at the stranger with a little curiosity. He finished at length, and then, taking one of the Captain's pipes, without asking leave, filled it with tobacco, lit it, and began to smoke and to talk in an easy companionable way.

"Yes," he said complacently, "I'm a convict. One-and-twenty years I got. And if I'm caught, it will be a life sentence, I dessay—with a flogging. I've had nearly a year, and might have got out six months ago, but it was a pity not to let the Chaplain have a chance. Pro-fesh burglar. Cracker of cribs. That's what I am. Bagger of swag. That is my calling—it hath bin." I thing he persuaded himself that he was quoting from the poets, because he repeated the line : "That is my calling—it hath bin. I was lagged last summer for a little business

in the country, and came down here with a few
other gentlemen, also in misfortune, to work out
the one-and-twenty years.

" One-and-twenty years! What do they think
of it, them Beaks and the Wigs? One-and-twenty
years! It drops out as glib as—as—this here rum
and water. Home they goes to their port wine
and their sherry wine, and off we goes to the
skilly and water. One-and-twenty years! Why
don't they take and hang a man at once? Well—
see here, now, there ain't a crib, not one solitary
crib you can pint to in this blessed world that I
can't crack. And so I've cracked even that convict crib that they thought to make so precious
tight. Cracked it, I did, like—like—a egg; and
here I am. First, aboard a hulk. That's poor
work, because you've got to swim ashore when you
do get out, and when you are ashore what's a man
worth in wet clothes? Besides, I can't swim. If
everybody knew what was comin' in the future,
everybody 'ud learn to swim. As long as I was
aboard that hulk I was sad. Seemed as if a fellow
hadn't got a chance. When we come ashore, I
began to pick up my spirits, looked all about, and

I made up my little plan at wunst, and after a month or two—picking up a nail here and a nail there, and havin' the use of my fingers, as one may say, and not being altogether a bloomin' idiot— why—here I am."

"Yes," said Leonard, "you certainly are here. But, as we don't care about the society of burglars and escaped convicts, perhaps you will go on to say what you have to say, and relieve us of your company."

"Quite right, my noble lord," replied the burglarious professor, cheerfully. "Quite right, and just what I should have expected of such an' out an' out tip-top swell as you. It ain't the society you're accustomed to, is it? And yet you can't, I should say, as a general rule be fond of entertainin' slaughterers and killerers, can you? Now what I've got to say is just this here. I see the whole fight from the beginnin' to the end. Where was I? Curled up in the shade I was, behind a tree, wishing that there moon"—here he used a strong adjective which, with other strong adjectives, I suppress, even though their absence detracts from the fidelity of the story and the splendour of the style—" would hide her face behind a cloud. Then a fellow might ha' had a chance. There *is* a 'ouse in this town which I knows of, where I'd a bin taken in and kep' secret and comfortable for a bit, perhaps—naterally I wanted to get to that 'ouse. A moonlight night and the month o' June, without a atom of real dark. Ah! give me a good December night; as black as your hat; and a sweet crib to crack in the country, with on'y a woman or two in the place. Dear me!—Well, gents both, as I was a-lying there, wishin', as I said—I see a brace o' men get over the gate and make for the middle of the field."

"Three men," said Wassielewski, "and a lady. Two were spirits."

"Now, don't you interrupt, mate. I know nothink about spirits. I ses to myself, 'What's up?' I ses. 'Cause somethink was bound to be up when two men gets into a field a midnight and stand face to face in the moonlight. 'It can't be,' I ses, 'that there looking after Stepney Bob'— that's me, gents both, 'cos he ain't missed yet, and won't be missed before five o'clock in the morning. So I concluded to keep quiet and see. Next moment, one of 'em chucks his hat and cloak—this hat and this cloak—on the grass, and then I see the two knives flash in the moonlight, and the fight began. One was a tall thin man with long white hair—that was you, mate—and t'other was a tall stout man with short white hair. That's the dead un—him as owned this cloak and this hat.

"I *have* seen 'em fight at the Whitechapel Theayter—one, two, three, give and take, while the music plays—and I don't suppose there's a properer way of getting through a long evening than the gallery of that 'ouse when there's a good fightin' piece on. But such a fight as this here I never see before on no boards whatsumever. For one, he began to cuss and swear, and danced about flourishing his knife, making lunges—like that"— the gentleman illustrated his narrative with a supper-knife—"and never managed to hit the t'other at all. Reg'lar wild he looked. Couldn't fight proper for rage. Lor'! put such a chap as that before Ben Caunt, and where'd he be in a pig's whisper? Never done no mischief with *his* knife. The t'other, this here old cove—there now, it was a real treat to see him. The moon was

in his face so as I should have thought it
blinded him ; but he took no notice ; only looked
his man straight in the eyes—that's the trick that
does it—never said ne'er a word, and kept on
parryin' them lunges quiet and beautiful—like
this "—more illustration with the knife.

"A matter of six minutes it might have lasted,
that fight, or perhaps ten, because you don't count
the time when you're lookin' at a fight. And then
all of a sudden like, I see this same old cove put
out his fist with the knife in it—and the t'other
falls back upon the grass. That was all, wasn't it,
mate? He got up once on his arm, but he fell
back again. And he was dead, wasn't he, mate?"

He stopped to take breath and another pull of
the rum and water.

"Another dollop o' that cold ham on the sideboard, little gunner, would be very grateful, it
would indeed, after the patter. Thank ye kindly.
Now I'm better."

He actually devoured another plateful of ham
before he would go on again.

"Well, what I came for to say is this here. After
the t'other un rolled over I see the old cock here

walk up and down the meadow slow, as if he was thinkin' what to do next. 'Why don't he bolt?' I ses. 'Why don't he clear his pockets?'"

"I was walking to the gate with Roman Pulaski," explained Wassielewski.

"No—not a bit—never went near his pockets. He goes on walkin' up and walkin' down, mutterin' with his lips. Presently he makes for the palin's. I instantly begins to crawl through the grass. When he got over the rails and walked away I was free to look after the t'other. Quite dead he was, dead as a door-nail."

"The Lord delivered him into my hands," said Wassielewski.

"And then I saw what a blessed Providential Go it was for me," the convict went on. "First I picked up his cloak, this most beautiful cloak, which you see goes right down to my heels, and covers up the uniform lovely. Then I picked up this here hat, which is a tile as good as new, and fits me like as if it was made for my head and not for his'n. A better tile I never swagged. Then I remembered that, if I had a little money, it wouldn't be a bad thing. So I searched his pockets. There was a

purse and there was a lot of letters and papers. I
left the letters and I opened the purse. Twelve
golden sovereigns and some notes—for I won't
deceive you, gents both. What d'ye think I did?
I ses to myself, 'If they bring it in murder agin
the old un, they shan't bring it in robbery too, 'cos
robbery is one thing and murder's another. These
two things ought never to be com-bined.' I ought
to know, 'cos I've cracked cribs since I was big
enough to walk, and might ha' murdered dozens of
innocent and confiding women, asleep in their beds.
But I never did. No, never. So I takes all the
sovereigns in the purse, and in his waistcoat pocket
I leaves three or four shillin's, and I leaves all the
rest, the flimsies, a lovely gold watch, a sweet
chain, and a diamond ring. It went to my 'art not
to have 'em, but I thought of this jolly old game
rooster, and I left 'em."

"Chivalry," said Leonard, "is always a pleasant
thing to meet with, even—go on, most excellent
burglar."

"The knife was in him, and his own knife was in
his hand. What do you think I done next? I
takes the knife out of the wound, and sticks it in

his hand, 'stead of his own. And I've brought along his own, and here it is."

He laid the knife upon the table—it was a long pointed knife, like a stiletto—of foreign shape and make. I did not ask Wassielewski if it was his, but gave it to Leonard. "One more thing," this philanthropist went on, "one more thing I done. There were marks of feet, and the grass was trampled. So I dragged him away, and laid him under the trees at the side of the field. They'll never think of looking in the middle and finding marks of a fight. After all that, I shouldn't wonder —I rally shouldn't—if they brought it in a Fellar D. C. But my advice to you, a game old cock as deserves to get off and die in the sheets, a laughin' at 'em all, is this, Whatever the werdict, you up and leg it, and then bring in a *alibi*. You ain't the sort to get off in a hurry ; you walked so precious slow down the street that I had time to do all that and catch you up before ever you got out o' sight. I dodged yer all the way here, and sneaked in after you. 'Cos, I ses, I'd like to let him sleep comfortable if I could, ses I."

After all, one could not but feel grateful to this

enthusiastic lover of a fight, in spite of the horrible circumstances of the case, and the tragedy which had just taken place. Somehow its outlines looked less horrible told by this gaol-bird than when Wassielewski related the story.

"And now I'll go," he said, getting up, and wrapping his cloak about him, "I can tramp it up to London, and hide all the day somewheres. No one won't suspect Stepney Bob beneath this miling-tary cloak and this out-an-out tile. Once back in Whitechapel, I know a place or two where they won't nab me for a spell, I don't think, and p'raps I'll step it altogether. And then you'll, may be, hear of me cracking cribs for the Americans. Good-night, gents both. Good-night, matey. Don't ye be down on your luck. But take my advice and leg it."

"Stay," said Leonard. "It's a delicate thing, interfering with your arrangements, and one's actions might be misunderstood, but if I might advise——"

"Go on, guv'ner."

"I would suggest that if you are not missed you will not be suspected, and a first-class traveller to

London by the mail train at one-thirty, disguised, as you say, in that excellent cloak, would have a better chance of reaching Whitechapel safely than a tramp."

Stepney Bob was struck with the suggestion.

"That's true," he said thoughtfully. "The train 'ud be in by four, and I shan't be missed till five. And in case o' accidents, I suppose"—he looked hard at Wassielewski—"I suppose that there ain't no one here who'd be so generous and so werry thoughtful as to step half a mile out o' the town and take a pair o' shears, and nip they strong adjectived telegraph wires. Now, that 'ud be a job worth braggin' about. Come now, they'd make a song out o' that job, I'd bet a trifle, and you'd be sung up and down the streets; all Whitechapel should ring with it, and the Dials too, and Ratcliffe Highway. Think o' that, mate."

No one volunteered to cut the telegraph wires, and after a little more rum and water Stepney Bob decided on going, and disappeared after a cautious inspection of the street.

"It would read sweetly in the paper, wouldn't

it," said Leonard, "how Captain Copleston and Ladislas Pulaski spent the night in assisting the escape of a convicted burglar, known in the Profession as Stepney Bob—however——"

"And what will you do, Wassielewski?"

"I shall do nothing. My work is over. I shall start for Poland—to-morrow. Ladislas Pulaski, if you marry and have children, teach them always that they are Poles. I was wrong in trying to get you with us. I see now that I was wrong. You will never fight for Poland. Another life is yours. God bless it for you—for the dear memory of your mother."

He laid his hand upon my head, rested it there for a few moments, and then went away, walking slowly and heavily, as if wearied with the weight of his life's work.

"Bear up, Laddy," said Leonard. "Come—be a man—poor old Wassielewski is not responsible for his actions. Go to bed, and to-morrow we will act."

"I feel somehow as if the blood of that man was on my head, Leonard. It is through me that he was detected."

"Some people would say that the finger of Fate was in it, Laddy—I say that it is a fitting end to a life of spying, watching, and informing. I wish all secret service agents could be got rid of in a similar way. Meantime, we must wait for to-morrow—I must think what we had better do."

"I cannot go upstairs, Leonard. I feel as if that dead body were lying in my room, waiting for me. Do not leave me to-night."

I could not bear to be alone. My nerves were like cords tingling and vibrating. I was in the presence of death and the other world. My brain was reeling.

Leonard carried me upstairs, I think, and laid me on the bed, when presently, while he sat beside me, as if I was a sick girl, I fell into a deep sleep, and dreamed that Wassielewski and I were trudging together along a road which I knew to be in Poland, and that before us stood our home—a stately mansion—and on the steps were Roman and Claudia Pulaski, holding out arms of welcome. And as I looked, Wassielewski suddenly left me, and I was alone. But he had joined the other two, and now all three were standing together waiting for me. Whenever, now, I dream of the past or of that fatal day, it is to see those three waiting still for me to join them.

.

CHAPTER XIII.

A CORONER'S INQUEST.

It is a shame for a man to have to confess his own weakness ; but the truth has to be told. I broke down at this point, and lay on the bed to which Leonard carried me for three weeks, in delirium. I suppose the great horror and shock of the evening, following on the nervous agitation of the preceding three days, was more than my brain could bear. At any rate, I had a bad time for the next fortnight or so, during which things went on without my being interested in them. Could one remember what delirium means, a chapter might be written—but one would need to be De Quincey to write it. First the chest seems to expand, and then the head to swell out and become of gigantic size. Then you lay your hands upon the forehead to make sure that it has not been carried somewhere else. Then you grow big all over, hands and feet and limbs. Then you lose all sense of weight, and seem to be flying in the air. And then, just as you are beginning to feel uncomfortable, your mind runs away from your control: things grotesque, things splendid, things absurd, things of the past, things from books, wild imaginations crowd the brain, and move before the eyes like a real pageant of living creatures. Nothing astonishes, nothing seems strange; there is no sense of incongruity, and when you recover all is forgotten but the general impression of grotesque unreality. They told me afterwards what had happened.

They discovered, early in the morning, two things. First that a convict had escaped, and secondly that a dead man was lying in the meadow beneath the walls.

At first they connected the two things, but subsequent inquiry led them to believe that the convict had nothing to do with the homicide.

As soon as Leonard could leave me with the

Captain he sought the old Pole. Wassielewski's single room was on the second floor in one of the crowded streets near Victory Row. The sailor's wives were all gathered about their doors, though the rain was falling heavily, talking of the discovery of the dead body, and wondering whether it was a murder or only a suicide. Most of them knew Leonard as an old inhabitant of the *quartier*, and saluted him kindly as Gentleman Jack, a name which they learned from their husbands' friends, the soldiers.

Leonard asked if the old man had been seen that morning. He had not, it was too early in the morning. It was his custom to remain in his room until noon, unless he was engaged to play for a paid-off crew. At twelve he descended, and would seldom return home till the evening. Leonard would find him in his room.

He mounted the stairs, and knocked. There was no answer. He knocked again. Again there was no answer. Could he have gone off already, on his way to Poland, acting on the burglar's advice?

Leonard went down the stairs again, and asked the mistress of the house. No, he had not gone

out.   He came home late, she said, perhaps as late
as twelve, because she must have been in bed some
time, and his footsteps woke her; but she had
been up since six, and he certainly had not come
downstairs.

She came up with Leonard this time, and they
both knocked.

Then they called him by his name.

All was still and silent.

Leonard leaned his shoulder against the door and
pushed.   The bolt came away from the rotten
wood, and the door fell open.

Wassielewski was kneeling by the bedside.   In
his hands was the miniature of my mother, and his
lips were pressed closely to it.   But the lips were
as hard and as cold as the hands that held the cross,
for the poor old man was dead.

He was not undressed.   He died in his devotions,
perhaps immediately after he came home.   Red-
handed with the blood of the spy, he went unrepentant to the after world.   The two souls, side
by side, departed almost together.

This event, as Leonard said, simplified matters
amazingly.   It was no longer necessary for him to

consider how the old man ought to give himself up
to justice. It seemed pretty clear that the convict
would hold his tongue, even if he got caught, while
if he got away he would certainly tell nothing.
On the other hand, if he did tell, it would be time
enough to reveal the real truth. There was excuse,
at any rate, in the plea that, the old Pole being
dead, nothing could be gained by letting the world
know that, like Lamech, he had slain a man.

The inquest on Wassielewski was very short.
He had been found dead, he was an aged man, the
doctor certified that the cause of death was
disease of the heart, the verdict was given in accord-
ance with the evidence, and the poor old man was
buried with the rites of his own Church.

By common consent of the few Poles who remained in the town, Leonard took possession for
me of the few effects which the old man left.
There were two or three weapons, relics of the last
struggle, and his violin. We looked through the
drawers and cupboard, but there were only a few
papers containing lists of names and plans of campaigns. These were burnt to prevent accidents.
Also there was a bag full of sovereigns—seventy or

eighty—which he had put together in readiness for a start at a moment's notice. With the Captain's consent, and by his advice, I subsequently distributed the legacy among his fellow-countrymen, who all came to the funeral of the most determined patriot that ever Poland produced.

A more important inquest was that held on the same day upon the body of Herr Räumer.

Ferdinand Brambler was, of course, present, taking notes with the air of one who has got hold of a good thing and means to make the most of it. Also he was himself conscious of an accession of importance, for was not the deceased a lodger in his brother Augustus's house ?

They first called the policeman who had found the body.

He deposed that early in the morning, at half-past four, he took the walk under the walls in the course of his beat, that he saw lying on the grass just within the meadow the body of a man. The man was dressed, but without a hat. Money was in his pocket—somehow the statement of Stepney Bob and that of the policeman did not exactly tally, and either the burglar helped himself to more than

he confessed, or the policeman took advantage of
the situation and took two notes, at least, on his
own account—that the deceased had upon him also
a watch and chain and a diamond ring, those,
namely, that lay on the table.

A suspicious juror—there is always, I believe, a
suspicious juror—here requested to see the watch
and chain, which he inspected minutely. The deceased lay, the policeman went on, as if he had
fallen backwards after the blow was inflicted, and
never moved again. The knife, which was that
lying on the table, was of foreign make, such as a
German gentleman might have carried. Being
asked if he thought it was a murder, he said that
there were no marks of violence or trampling in
the grass, that, as he had not been robbed, he
did not see why it should have been a murder.
That from the knife being held tight in the right
hand he thought it was suicide.

Then the doctor was called, the same doctor who
gave evidence in the case of Wassielewski. He
stated that death had been caused by a deep
wound which punctured right through the heart,
that the death must have been instantaneous ; that

although such a wound would require the greatest determination, it was quite possible for a man to inflict it upon himself; that the right hand tightly held a knife covered with blood, and that the wound, in his opinion, was undoubtedly inflicted by that knife, the one before the jury.

The next witness was Mr. George Tyrrell, the Mayor of the Borough. He deposed that Herr Carl Räumer and himself were on friendly and intimate terms: that he had the management of his affairs; that he knew nothing whatever of his family connections in Germany; that a short time previously the Herr had instructed him to realise certain investments, which had been done as he requested; that he had last seen the deceased on the morning of his death, when nothing whatever passed which could warrant a belief that he was about to commit suicide; that, on the contrary, he stated he was about to go away to the Continent, there to take up his permanent residence. But, on the other hand, he had received a note in the evening which struck him as singular. This note he would read. It was short, and was as follows:

"DEAR TYRRELL,

"I find that my departure will take place earlier than I intended. I wished to see you again, I shall, however, go this night and for ever. My affairs are all settled. I wish, as you will never see me again, that you will take care of Ladislas Pulaski. Do not let the boy be persuaded ever to go to Poland. That is my solemn advice to him. Yours,

"C. R."

He said that on the receipt of the letter he thought at first of going round, but as the hour was late he refrained, to his present great regret. The letter was brought by a child, daughter of his clerk, Augustus Brambler, in whose house Herr Räumer lodged.

The Coroner asked if any of the jury wished to put any questions to His Worship the Mayor. The suspicious juror wished to ask the Mayor if he was quite certain about the hand-writing. The Mayor had no doubt whatever of the letter being in his old friend's writing.

Then Charlotte Brambler was called. The report in the paper of the following Saturday, with which, of course, Ferdinand Brambler had nothing to do, spoke of her as a most intelligent, straightforward witness, who gave her evidence clearly and to the point. "Her face," the report went on, "is singularly attractive, and her appearance and demeanour elicited universal respect and admiration. She is, we understand, the eldest, not the second daughter, as reported, of Mr. Augustus Brambler, long and honourably connected with the Legal interests of the Borough."

Little Forty-four did give her evidence very well. She had to say that she attended to Herr Räumer, and that at nine o'clock in the evening he called her up, and sent her with a letter to Mr. Tyrrell. There was no answer, and she returned immediately after delivering the note. Then he rang the bell again and told her that he was going away that night—going on a long journey.

An intelligent juror here interposed. He said that a long journey might mean anything, and he asked the witness why she did not ask him how long it was?

Forty-four replied that she never asked Herr Räumer anything, but answered his questions, and as he did not say where he was going, it was not for her to inquire. She went on to depose that he added that he should not return any more; that instead of a month's notice he paid down a month's rent; that as she had attended him for some years he gave her a five-pound note, which he advised her to keep for herself, and not waste it in buying things for her brothers and sisters—this was a touch entirely Räumeresque. Then he looked about the room, and said that the furniture could go to Mrs. Brambler, and she might have his old piano if she liked. Then she asked him what they were to do with the books which are in French, with yellow paper covers, in fact, French novels. He laughed, and said that if she pleased she might keep them till her brothers grew up, and then give them the books, which would certainly teach them a good deal about life previously unsuspected by them; but that, if she preferred, she might sell them for what they would fetch as waste paper. At all events, he would never want any of the books or any of the things any more.

The Coroner here interposed, and asked her if

she was quite sure that those were the very words the lodger used.

The witness was perfectly certain that those were his exact words.

"He would never want the books or any of the things any more."

The jury whispered together.

Then the Coroner asked the girl about the knife.

She knew nothing about the knife; she had never seen such a knife in his room ; but could not swear that he had no such knife, because he kept everything locked up. Perhaps the knife had been lying among Herr Räumer's things in one of the drawers. Had never tried to look into the drawers, would not be so mean as to pry into things.

Here the suspicious juror remarked plaintively that he should like to see the five-pound note which the deceased had given her. She produced the note, which was handed round among the jury, who examined it as carefully as if it had been an important *pièce de conviction.* Then they all shook their heads at one another, and gave it back to the Coroner, who restored it to Forty-four.

There being no other evidence to call, the Coroner proceeded to sum up.

The jury must consider, he said, all the circumstances. The deceased informed an old friend in the morning that he intended to go away shortly; in the evening he sent a very extraordinary epistle, stating that he was going away "for ever"—the jury would make a note of that expression. At the same time he tells the little girl who was accustomed to attend upon him—and he was constrained to express his admiration at the very straightforward way in which that little girl's evidence was given—that he was going away, and was not coming back again. Let the jury mark, at this point, the suddenness of resolution. He took nothing with him; he abandoned the piano, his books, everything; and even made the very important remark that he should not want any of them any more. Why not? If a man goes on the Continent he does not give up reading; if a man changes his residence he does not throw away, so to speak, all his furniture, but carries it with him, or sells it; but Herr Räumer was not, as he told the girl, Charlotte Brambler, going on the

Continent; he was going—let the jury mark this very earnestly, he was going—on a long journey. Very good: but consider another point. The doctor was of opinion that the blow, if that of a suicide, must have required great determination. Possibly, perhaps, Herr Räumer had not the requisite amount of resolution, but the jury all remembered him—a stout, stern, and determined-looking person. As to courage, no man could tell when any other man's courage came to an end. And there were the facts that the knife was found in his hand, covered with blood; that there was no sign of any struggle on the ground, and that the knife was of foreign manufacture. If it was not suicide, what was it? Could the jury believe that a man of singularly quiet, regular, and reserved habits, should go out in the dead of the night, after making those remarkable statements and writing that remarkable letter, for a stroll, without his hat, on the walls? That he should then, still with the intention of taking a purposeless stroll, have climbed over the wooden railings into the field, and then presented his breast, offering no resistance, to the murderer? Then it was whispered that a convict escaped that morning from the prison close by might have done the deed. First of all, he must say that it appeared to him disgraceful that any convict should escape, but it was absurd to connect the convict with the death of a man he could not have known, and whom he did not rob. Also, how did that convict get hold of a foreign knife? Let the police catch and produce the fugitive, and it would then be time to consider the absurd suggestion. There, in fact, was the evidence, all before the jury. They were a body of educated and intelligent men; they had sat at Coroners' inquests before, and he, the Coroner, was glad to say that a more trustworthy body of men to weigh evidence impartially he did not hope or desire to find. He therefore dismissed them in the confident hope that they would shortly return with a verdict.

In five minutes the jury came back. Their finding was unanimous. It was that the deceased committed suicide while suffering from temporary insanity.

This verdict, never disputed, was the end of the whole business. The deceased was buried at the expense of the Mayor, who acted as chief mourner.

Our Polish friends made not the slightest sign of any knowledge of the deed; no one in the town knew anything, and our only accomplice was Stepney Bob. I never heard that he was re-captured, and I have every reason to believe that he managed to escape altogether and get to America or some other part of the world, where his possible good private qualities had not been obscured by his public reputation as a cracker of cribs. Nor did it appear that any inquiry was made into the matter by the Russians. They did not acknow-ledge the *mouchard* who died fighting for his life with one of the people whom he was paid to watch. If he had friends or relations, none of them ever turned up. No doubt his was an assumed name, under which no one of his own people would be likely to recognise him.

When I recovered, and was able to be told everything, I confess to a feeling that fortune for once had found a fitting death for a man.

We never told the Captain, Leonard and I. But once, when Mr. Tyrrell had been lamenting in public over his great private loss, while he was perfectly oblivious of the little facts which preceded the death of his friend, I ventured to tell him privately the whole history. After that we never mentioned him again. The behaviour of Leonard in suppressing the real facts was, like his conduct when first he introduced himself to the Captain—what Mr. John Pontifex called a Wrong Thing.

CHAPTER XIV.

"LEONARD AND CIS."

I GOT well again and strong, but I was forbidden to do any teaching work for two or three months, and had to give up all engagements for that space.

A holiday of three months, with Celia to come every day, till I was strong enough to go out, and read to me; the Captain to fidget about what was best for me to eat and drink; Leonard to tell stories, and sometimes the Rev. John Pontifex to come and sit with me, making profound remarks on the wickedness of men in general, his own Fearful backslidings in his youth, and the incredible amount of repentance which they involved, the ignorance of the Papists, and the strength of will possessed by his remarkable wife. Or Mr. Broughton,

who would come round, and, by way of giving me
a fillip, read a little Greek with me and then send
round a few bottles of choice old Port. Mrs. Pontifex sent strawberries and tracts; she also told me
that my fever was no doubt intended to bring me
more directly under the influence of her husband's
ministrations. Augustus Brambler would come
bursting in between the intervals of writ-serving
and message-running, to tell me joyfully of the
great business done by the House. And little
Forty-four would come as often as she could; if no
one else was with me she sat down, beaming with
smiles, the tenderest of little nurses, and told me
how they were all getting on,—Forty-six developing
into a real genius over his books—he was the son
who subsequently became a Reporter and Journalist;
Forty-eight, who had been caned at school for in-
subordination, and so on. I learned, too, from her
that the famous five-pound note had been, contrary
to the donor's intention, distributed in new clothes,
as far as it would go, among the whole family. A
new lodger had been found who was at least more
considerate than the former, did not dine at home,
and talked to the children.

But, of course, Celia was the most regular visitor, and with her, Leonard. They came together, and went away together; and in my presence he made shameless love till sometimes the light of answering love flashed for a moment in her eyes, and then she drew herself from him, blushing, and fell to busying about my pillows. Miss Rutherford drove over from Fareham, too. She turned out to be exactly what she looked at first sight—for that matter, people always do : a gentle, quiet, and careful old lady, who ought to belong to some planet where there are no such things as temptations, follies, or worldliness. She was always prettily and daintily dressed, and as became an elderly lady, behind the fashion.

She had a sweet and pleasant face, with an expression on it which reminded one of Leonard, and when she spoke it was in a clear and precise way, like the ripple of a stream over stones. And when she looked at her nephew it was with an ever-growing wonder that there should be in the world such a boy as that to call her Aunt.

Imagine all the sentimental and tender things that these two women, Miss Rutherford and Cis, would say to each other and to me as they sat beside my arm-chair while I was recovering. Think, if you can, how they were bound together by their common love for one man, and how they would read, as women always try to do, in each other's soul, dissatisfied until they succeed in finding, as in a mirror, each her own image in the heart of the other. Some women can have no half measures; they must love wholly and trust altogether; and they must receive back as much as they give.

I tried to write down some of these tender scenes, but I have torn them up; words that are altogether sweet and precious when spoken sometimes look sentimental and meaningless when they are written down. What they came to was this, that two women tried to spoil one man by attention and thoughtfulness, and did their best to make another man vain by their exceeding love for him. I do not think either was much injured.

In September we all four, Miss Rutherford acting chaperon, went to the Lakes together in order to complete my recovery.

I have been in many places since the year 1858, and enjoyed many holidays. I have learned to know this beautiful garden set with all manner of delights, with mountain, stream, lakes, and forests, with all kinds of sweet flowers and singing birds to raise the heart of man, which we call England. I have dreamed away the hours in the pleasant land of France, among old castles by the stately Loire, or where the white cliffs of Normandy face their sisters of Albion. I have sat among the students of Germany and wandered among the sweet-scented pines round mountain feet, but I have had no holiday such as that. A dreamy time, when one was still weak enough to allow the sentiment of the situation to dwell in the mind, with a clinging for the last time to the robe of Celia, while all sorts of sweet phrases and cadences gathered themselves together and took shape in my heart, to be expressed in music when I might find time to set them down, with a new interest in listening to the talk, so truthful and so old-fashioned, of the lady whom chance had joined to our party, who ought to have been set in a bower full of flowers and fruit, with pictures about her of angels—not Churchy angels —ladies could be pious twenty years ago without ecclesiastical rubbish—and faces of holy women full of trustful thought. With this, the old admiration for Leonard, the strong, the brave, the handsome Leonard.

One evening, after sunset, we were in a boat on Derwentwater, Leonard, Cis, and I. Leonard was rowing us gently, letting the oars dip slowly in the smooth water, and then resting, while the boat made slow way among the wooded islets. Cis and I sat side by side in the stern, she was steering. The dark foliage was black now, and the lighter leaves were changed into a dark green. The lake was still and quiet, now and then a fish came to the surface with an impatient splash as if it really was getting too dull down below; or a wild-fowl flew over our heads with a whirr; or a noise of voices, mellowed by distance, came across the water from the hotel, and far off somewhere a man was blowing a horn, and the echoes flew from hill to hill.

"'Blow, bugles, blow, set the wild echoes flying,'" Celia quoted softly.

And then we were all silent again.

It was Leonard who spoke next. Deeper darkness had fallen upon us now, clouds were coming up in the west, and the breeze began to rise. The boat was quite motionless, on either hand an islet, before us in the distance the lights of the hotel reflected in the water. And again the sweet rolling echoes of the horn.

Said Leonard, speaking slowly:

"There is a thing I should like to tell you, Cis, if Laddy will let me. It is a thing which he told me in his delirium, a thing I ought to have suspected before, but did not, so dull and selfish as I was. Can you guess what it is?"

I could guess very well. There was nothing else that I could have told unknown to Cis already.

"I thought I was the only one who knew," Leonard continued. "But I was not; the Captain knows."

"He knew before," I murmured. "Tell Cis, if you please, Leonard, if you think well. But remember, it is all a thing of the past—forgotten—torn up by the roots."

"When I went away, Cis, dear," Leonard began, "I left you in the charge of Ladislas. You were, I told him, in my conceited way, to be his peculiar trust, he was to look after you, to watch you, and to anticipate everything that you could want."

"And so he has done," said Cis. "Haven't you, Laddy?"

"The reason I gave him was that I loved you, my Queen, and that if things went well—all looks easy to a boy—I proposed coming back, and telling you myself—in five years' time. Observe, please, the extraordinary selfishness of a boy of eighteen. At that age one cannot possibly think of anything but oneself. Well—I went away—I came back. Fortune had been kinder to me—far kinder than I ever deserved. I am loaded with the gifts of Heaven. Don't think me ungrateful, because I talk little about these things. I can only talk of them to you two. But that is nothing. While I was away, Cis, you grew from a child into a woman."

"Yes, Leonard."

"What I did not think of was that Laddy was growing too from a boy to a man—what I forgot was that there would be one girl and two men— that both men might love the same girl."

"Laddy!" Cis cried with surprise and pain.

"Forgive me, Cis," I said, "Leonard has told you the truth. For a time—it was early this year, I think—what he hinted at was the case. I fought with it, and I beat it down, because it was hopeless, and because of the promise I gave to Leonard. But it is true that there was a time when I gave way, and—ventured to love you, otherwise than a brother may. Why did you tell her, Leonard?"

"Because I want her and myself to feel more what we owe to you, Laddy, to your unselfish labour, your watchfulness, and the sacrifice of your own interests. He loved you, and he gave you up, Cis. I wonder if any words of mine could make you understand what that meant to him."

"It could never have been, Leonard," I said. "How could it? Celia was my sister, always."

She laid her hand in mine and one arm upon my shoulder.

"Always your sister, Laddy dear. And henceforth more and more. There is now nothing that we have not told each other."

Henceforth, more and more. Yes, as the time has gone by, nothing has dimmed the steady trust and affection which Celia has showered upon me. I can see now, too, how different her life would have been, how wanting in fulness, had things been different, and had she married me. Some women are happiest with a man of action; how could the life of a dreamer like me satisfy the aspirations of a girl who worthily fills the place of Leonard's wife, and has stepped gracefully into the rank to which his success has raised her?

About that one thing we never spoke any more.

Leonard rowed us quietly back to the hotel, the lawn of which ran down to the water's edge. The garden was full of the visitors, for the evening was warm. They looked at us as we passed them, Celia with her hand on my shoulder in the old familiar fashion, staring with that half-impudent, furtive way in which English people at hotels look at each other and at strangers. In the *salon* was nobody but Miss Rutherford, quietly waiting our return.

She asked Leonard to take her into the garden for a walk, and left Celia and me alone.

Then I sat down to the piano, and collected my thoughts—all those musical thoughts of which I have spoken,—and began to play them.

It was no improvisation, because the ideas had been long in my head, and many of them had been already noted down and tried over, but it was the first time I played the piece as a whole.

"What is it, Laddy?" Celia asked, as she saw me striving to talk to her in the old fashion with my fingers on the keys, a language unknown to the outer world. "What is it? I cannot understand it yet."

"Listen, Cis. It is a love poem of two young people—we will call them 'Leonard and Cis.' It tells how one went away, and how after five years he came back again, not a prodigal son, but covered with honour; how they fell in love at once, and how after many difficulties, which were got over in a most surprising and extraordinary manner, quite as if these two lovers belonged to a novel, which, of course, they did not; and how they were finally married, and lived happily for ever and ever. Now listen."

The symphony came forth from my brain clear and distinct, and, after a few bars of prelude, flowed straight on to the end. I have written plenty of music since, though I am not, as Celia affects to think me, a great composer, but I have written none that has pleased me so much, that dwells so constantly in my mind, and where I have found such fulness of expression. It is, I am sure, by some such masterful wave of passion that the highest expression and the noblest conceptions are brought together in the brain, and great works are produced.

I could see in my own music—and Celia could see it as well—first a rippling movement showing the peace and sunshine of early maidenhood ; then the yearnings and unconscious reaching out of hands in thought for a fuller and richer life ; then the awakening of Love the glorious, like the awakening of Adam in the garden to look about with wonder, to walk with uncertainty, to feel his way in broad daylight, to fear lest it should be a dream, and that the vision should pass away, and all be nothingness again. Presently followed the growth of passion till it became a great river for strength. And, lastly, the Wedding Hymn of triumph.

"Do you understand it, Cis?" I asked. "It is meant for you, and written for you. I shall copy it all out, and give you a copy, as my wedding present."

"I think I understand—some of it," she replied, "How can your pupil understand it all at first?

Oh! Laddy, you have made me very humble to-night. How can men love women as they do? What are we, and what can we do, compared with them, that they should lavish such affection upon us?"

" Ask Leonard," I replied, laughing.

And outside the people were all listening in the garden. When I finished there was a general applause, as if I had been playing for them.

That night, an hour later, I heard below in the garden the voices of those who sat up still.

" Who was it playing?" asked a girl's voice. " He has a sweet face; it is a pity he is deformed."

" It is a certain Pulaski—Pole, I suppose. Patriot most likely. Count, of course, or Baron, or Duke"—this agreeable person was a man, perhaps the young lady's husband—" some adventurer, most likely, who goes about trying to pick up a rich English wife by his tale of misfortunes and his pianoforte-playing. To-night's performance was an exhibition. No doubt he wants to fascinate that extremely pretty girl, almost as pretty as some one else I could name."

" Nonsense, sir, a great deal prettier; and,

besides, she's engaged to the tall young man, who is a Captain Copleston and a Crimean officer. The old lady with them is a Miss Rutherford. She his aunt, and plays propriety. I do not know anything about the pianoforte-player."

"Well, I'm glad she is not going to marry a hunchback, pianoforte-playing Pole."

Listeners, as has been frequently observed, never hear any good of themselves. But I played no more at the Derwentwater hotel, because next day we returned southwards, and began all of us to prepare diligently for Celia's wedding.

CHAPTER XV.

"RING, WEDDING BELLS!"

I HAVE come to the end of my story, the only story I have to tell from my own experience. How should it end but with a wedding? There is no romance where there is no love; there is no pleasure in the contemplation of love unless it ends happily, and is crowned with orange blossoms; love is the chief happiness of life, as everybody knows—except, perhaps, John Pontifex—and has ever been completed by the wedding bells.

Ring, wedding bells, then; shake out the clashing music of your joy over all the fields, startle the farmer at his work, rouse the student at his desk, strike on the ear of the sailor out at sea, echo along the shore, mingle with the roar of the saluting guns to greet the ship's crew when they come home, so that they may know that during their three years' cruise the world's happiness has not altogether died away. Bring back to the old a memory of a day long gone by. Lift up the heart of the young with hope. Put ambitious thoughts of such a day of victory into the mind of the maidens who would like nothing better than to hear the bells ring for themselves on such a wedding morning, and walk in such a procession, decked with such white robes and such orange wreaths. May they ring for every one of our girls, so that not one shall miss the love of a man but those who are unworthy.

They were married in the old church, the parish church, a mile from the town.

It is a day at the end of October, a breezy day of autumn; the clouds are driving across the sky, light clouds which leave plenty of clear blue sky and sunshine; the leaves are lying all about the old churchyard, drifting in heaps against the head-stones and whirling round and round like unquiet spirits within the iron railings of the vaults; at the edge of the paupers' corner is a small new cross,

quite simple, which I have not seen before. It is
" In memory of Lucy, wife of Captain Richard
Copleston, late of Her Majesty's Tenth Regiment
of Dragoons, who died in this town in childbirth,
in her twenty-first year." Poor Lucy! Poor hap-
less victim of a selfish and cold-hearted villain! I
knew that Leonard would put up some monument
to his mother's memory, but he had not told me
that it was done already. Doubtless he wished it
to be there before his marriage.

The churchyard is full of people waiting to see
the wedding; the honest folk from Victory Row
are there. I shake hands with Jem Hex and his
wife and half-a-dozen more, who knew me in the
old days of Mrs. Jeram's guardianship. They care
less for the bride than for the bridegroom, these
denizens of Victory Row. That a boy, so to
speak, who used to run ragged about the logs on
the Hard, who played on their own doorsteps, who
was accustomed to fight Moses daily, and on small
provocation, before the sight of all; who actually,
only the other day, did not disdain to remember
the old time, and cowhided Moses again at the
Blue Anchor; that such a boy should have become

such a man was not, of course, unexpected, because out of Victory Row have come plenty of distinguished men—though not down in books—Nelson's bulldogs, mind you, and a few of Wellington's veterans. But that he should have developed to that height of greatness as to be a real Captain in the army, and come home to marry nothing short of the daughter of the Mayor, and her a lady as beautiful as the day—that was, if you please, something quite out of the common.

Here is the Captain, marching up the walk in uniform and epaulettes as becomes a great occasion. Fall back, good people, don't crowd the Captain. God bless the Captain! Is the Captain looking well to-day? And a happy day for him, too, if all's true that's said. Which if any credit is due to anybody for that boy turning out so well, it's due to the Captain. There was only one Captain for these people. Other persons held equal rank in the Navy, it is true; there were, for instance, Captain Luff, Captain Hardaport, Captain Bobstay—who was only a retired master with Captain's title—all living not far from Victory Row; but they had their names assigned to them as well as their titles—ours had not.   The old man, pleased to see so many people gathered together to do honour to him and his, stops and has a word to say to every one, and then goes on to the Church, where, he stands by the altar, and waits.

The Rev. John Pontifex and Mrs. Pontifex his wife.   The sailor-folk know nothing of them except as residents.   So they pass in the silence of respect, John Pontifex with his long-tail coat on, and a very voluminous white muffler round his neck.

The Rev. Verney Broughton.   He it is who is going to marry them.   Ah! quoth John Hex, and a right sort, too, as he *has* heard, either for a glass of wine, or for a marriage, or for a sermon.   From Oxford College, he is, and once taught Master Leonard a mort o' learning, which, no doubt, helped him agin them Rooshans.

Among the people, bustling here and there with importance, is the historiographer, Ferdinand Brambler, note-book in hand.   He goes into the church ; comes out and dashes down observations in his note-book on a tombstone ; listens to the people and jots down more observations, and then,

absorbed in meditations, is seen standing motionless, as if grappling for the mastery of language.
This is a great day for Ferdinand.

Round the church door are all the younger
members of the Brambler family, told off to strew
flowers at the feet of the bride. Augustus is with
them, bearing in his hands a pair of new white
cotton gloves, and an air of immense dignity.
These crowds, this ringing of bells, strewing of
flowers, and general excitement, all attest in his
eyes to the greatness and glory of the Legal.
Nothing in the ·Scholastic, not even a prize-giving,
ever came near it. All the children are dressed in
new clothes presented by the Captain, so that they
may do fitting honour to the occasion.

· Leonard had pressed me to be his best man,
which, indeed, was my proper place. But I wanted
to play the organ for Celia's marriage, and I had
promised myself to play my own Love Symphony,
which she alone knew. It was a fancy of mine.
Forty-four, my faithful little ally and friend, begged
to come with me to the organ-loft.

It is after eleven, and time to go up the stairs.
What are those heavy heels tramping in the aisle ?

They are Leonard's company, with, I believe, about half the regiment, come to see Gentleman Jack married. I remembered the faces of the rogues; they were at the Blue Anchor that night when he thrashed Moses, and made him give up the papers. Jem the organ-blower is in his place; Forty-four is by me to turn over the leaves. Stay one moment, Forty-four, let us look through the curtains again. There is Leonard going up the aisle. He is in uniform, as are his best men as officers of the Garrison—the young naval officer whom they call Grif, and a man of his own regiment. A brave show of scarlet and gold. His brother officers are mostly in the church, and the Colonel among them.

"There comes Uncle Ferdinand," says Forty-four. "Oh! how beautifully he will describe it!"

All are there but the bride. She is coming. Now, Forty-four, for Celia's Symphony.

The music rolls and echoes among the rafters in the roof. As I play I am a prophet, and see before me the happy years unfold their golden wings. All is as it ought to be; let those who have to sit during their lives outside the halls of human joy take pleasure in the prospect of others' happiness, and be thankful that they can at least look on.

" There is the bride," whispered Forty-four. "Oh ! how lovely—oh ! how sweet she looks !"

My Wedding Hymn of Prayer and Praise—listen to it, Celia—I know that you are listening—as you stand for a moment before the altar beside your lover waiting for the words to be spoken. Listen. There is no joy, says the music, given to men and women like the holy joy of love ; there can be no praise too full and deep for the gift of love ; there can be no prayer too eloquent than the prayer for the continuance of love. Listen ! it is the voice of your heart speaking in the music which rings and rolls about the pillars of the old church—I learned it reading in your heart itself—it is singing aloud to God in gratitude and praise, singing in the music where I have enshrined it and preserved it for you.

I finish my symphony, and the service begins. The words are faint and low as they mount to the organ-loft. I have pulled the curtains aside, and we watch, we three, Forty-four, Jem the organ-blower, and I, from our gallery, while Leonard

holds Celia's hand in his, and they take the vow·
which binds them for ever to each other.   You are
crying, Forty-four ?   Foolish child.

All is over, and they have gone into the vestry.
Come, we have played Celia's Symphony before
the wedding with her Hymn.   Now for the March.
Mendelssohn alone has reached the true triumphal
rapture.   His music is the exultation of the bridegroom ; it is a man's song : the song of a man who
bears his bride away ; the song of the young men
who clap their hands ; the jubilant blare of cannons
and trumpets which throw their music abroad to
the winds that envious men may hear ; and though
the women cry, like foolish little Forty-four, we
·drown their tears with song and shout.   A bridegroom's song of triumph this.

But the bride is gone, and the bridal company
with her ; the children have strewn their flowers
upon the ground ; the carriages have driven off ;
only the people are left ; they, too, are leaving the
church ; in a few moments we shall be alone in the
loft. ·

Consummatum est.   Leonard has come home ;
Leonard has won his bride ; Celia has gone from

us. Shut up the organ, Forty-four; let us go down
and join the wedding guests. Somehow I do not
feel much like feasting.

Mr. Tyrrell was by no means the kind of man to
make a mean show on this auspicious occasion. He
had a marquee erected in his garden, where two
tables were laid; he invited to the breakfast his whole
staff of clerks with their families, including all who
bore the name of Brambler—they had the second
table; he would have invited all the regiment if Leonard had allowed him. As it was, there appeared a
great gathering of his brother officers. No nobler
wedding breakfast, Ferdinand Brambler reported,
had ever before been witnessed in the town, and it
reflected, he said, the greatest credit on Mr. Honeybun, the eminent local confectioner and pastrycook,
who evinced on this occasion talents of an order inferior to none, not even Fortnum and Mason, the
purveyors of princes. It may be mentioned that
the occasion was one of which Ferdinand made
four columns and a half. The wedding report ran
to the butcher's bill for three whole weeks, and in-
cluded a small outstanding account with the green-

grocer, as Augustus himself told me. It was headed, "Wedding of the Mayor's only Daughter," in large type, and was divided into headed sections. Thus : "The Churchyard," "Decorations of the Church," "The Organist," of whom he spoke with some reticence, for Ferdinand had feeling for my long friendship with bride and bridegroom ; "The Bridegroom and his Gallant Supporters," the "Arrival of the Bride," "The Wedding," in which he gave the rein to religious feelings, and spoke of the impressive reading of Mr. Broughton, the reverent attention of those war-stained heroes, the officers of the regiment, and the tears of the bridesmaids ; "The Departure," in which my own rendering of the "Wedding March" was gracefully alluded to ; and, finally, the "Wedding Breakfast," in the description of which he surpassed himself, so that those who read of that magnificent feed felt hungry immediately. I do not know what reward he received of Mr. Honeybun, the confectioner, but he ought to have had free run among the tarts for life. It was not at all a solemn or a tearful meal. Mr. John Pontifex, seated well out of his wife's sight, was between two young officers, to whom he communicated recollections of his early life at Oxford, and the reckless profligacy which he had witnessed, and even—"Oh!" I heard him say, "it is a most awful event to look back upon"—participated in and encouraged. He told them the Goose story, he told how he had once fallen in love with a young person—in fact, of the opposite sex—in Oxford, and how, excepting that single experience, "Love," as he said, "has never yet, I regret to say, reached this poor—cold—heart of mine." All this was very delightful to his two hearers, and I observed the rapture with which they plied him with champagne, of which he drank immense quantities, becoming frightfully pale, and listened to his reminiscences. No doubt Mrs. Pontifex would have been greatly pleased had she been present that evening in the mess-room, and heard the reproduction of these anecdotes. It was in the ponderous manner peculiar to clergymen of his standing and scholarship that Mr. Broughton proposed the health of the bride and bridegroom. He had known them both, he said, from infancy. There were no words at his command strong enough to express his affection for the bride, or, if he might

say so as a Christian man, his envy of the bridegroom.   On the other hand, for such a bride, there
was none fitter than such a bridegroom.   This
young Achilles, having obtained from the gods a
better fate than the hero to whom he likened him,
had returned victorious from the wars, and won
the fairest prize.   They all knew Leonard Copleston's history, how the young gentleman, the son
of a long line of gallant gentlemen, met adverse
fortune with a resolute front, and conquered her,
not with a sword, but with a bayonet; what they
did not know, perhaps, was what he could tell
them, as Leonard's tutor, that he had always as a
boy looked on the gallant soldier as the noblest
type of manhood.   "We all," said Mr. Broughton,
"envy the man who fights; even the most popular
priest is the priest militant; the glory of a poet or
a painter is pale compared with the glory of a
general; let us wish for Leonard Copleston a long
career of honour and distinction, and for them both,
my friends, for Leonard and Celia Copleston, let
us wish that their love may endure beyond the
brief moon of passion, and grow in depth as the
years run on; that in fact, like the finest Port, age

may only develop its colour, bring out its bouquet, and mature its character."

The old Captain would not speak, though they drank his health. He had been sitting opposite to Celia, and when they said kind things about him—it was Leonard's Colonel who said them—he only got up, and with a breaking voice said that he thanked God for the happiest day in all his life.

CHAPTER XVI.

CONCLUSION.

" Draw the curtains, Mrs. Jeram ; we will shut out the night. I will light the candles."

It is nearly twenty years later than Celia's wedding. Mrs. Jeram is an old woman now, and blind, but it pleases her to do little things, and to fancy that she is still housekeeper.

Everything is changed in the town. They have pulled down the old walls and levelled the moats ; the Dockyard has spread itself over the place where from Celia's Arbour we looked across the harbour. All the romance went out of the place when they swept away the walls and filled up the moats ; it was a cruel thing to do, but no one seemed to remonstrate, and it is done now. The Government

wanted the ground, they said. There was plenty
of other ground lying about, which they might
have had. The Milldam is filled up, and a soldiers'
hospital has been built upon it ; of course, the
King's Mill has gone too. All the old guard-
houses have been taken down ; the gates are no
longer 'shut at night ; in fact, there are no more
gates to shut. The harbour, too, is not what it
was ; they have wantonly broken up and destroyed
nearly all the old historic ships, save the one where
Nelson died, and she is as naked and as empty as
when she first came out of dock ; only a few of the
venerable hulks remain, and I dare say, while I am
writing these very lines, some economic Lord of
the Admiralty is issuing orders for the destruction
of the rest. The veterans with their wooden legs
have all left the bench upon the Hard, and gone to
the churchyard. The very bench is gone ; steam
launches run about the harbour to the detriment
and loss of the boatmen ; and a railway runs down
to the edge of the water. No doubt the improve-
ments were wanted, but still one regrets the past.
Of course, the sailor of the present is not like the
sailor of the past ; that we all know, and there is

little room for sorrow on that score. A new suburb has grown up behind our old wild and desolate sea-shore; it is a fine place, and we are proud of it. We are all changed together with our surroundings, and the *vie de province* is no longer what it was in the days of Mr. Broughton and the Captain. As for me, I have not changed. I am still a music-master. As I said at the beginning, you may read on my brass plate the name of "L. Pulaski, Teacher of Music and Singing." And people have quite left off the little confidential whisper, "a Pole of illustrious family—might enjoy a title if he wished." I have made a little name, not much, by certain things I have written, especially the Symphony I wrote for Celia—the best piece I have ever done. Mrs. Jeram, as I have said, lives with me still, and talks about the old, old days. She is sitting before me now as I write. See—I leave the table, and open the piano. The tears come into her darkened eyes.

"It is the tune the Captain liked," she says.

"To be sure it is.

"'The wind that blows, and the ship that goes,
And the lass that loves a sailor.'"

Almost needless to say that the old actors in the drama of my life are all dead.

The first to go was Mrs. Pontifex. She was, in her way fond of me, and I should have been guilty of ingratitude if, in return, I had not conceived a respect for her. As I think of her, so gaunt, so unbending in principles and shoulders, so upright in morals and in backbone, so unyielding in doctrine and in muffins, I wonder if I am already only forty, since she has left no one like her, and her race is extinct. She died of a cold caught through her adherence to one of her Christian privileges— never to light the fire in her sitting-rooms till November.

It was in 1860, a year about which I remember nothing except that it rained from June to October without stopping, and a wag announced in *Punch* that there would be no summer that year because the Zodiac was taken up for repairs. We all laughed at that, and then some of us began to reflect with shame, and especially those who had been educated by the Rev. Verney Broughton, that very likely it was true, and that certainly we had no sort of idea what the Zodiac was.

At the end of that continuous rain, then, Mrs. Pontifex died, and was gathered to her forefathers. A fortnight after I called on her husband. He was gardening, looking, as he stooped with his long thin figure over the plants, very much like a letter of the Hebrew alphabet.

He was weeding the strawberry bed—the strawberries that year by reason of the long rains had been like turnips for size and taste. He rose when he heard my footsteps, and shook his head solemnly. In either hand he held an apple. It struck me that this was the first proof of recovered liberty, as in his wife's time he had never been allowed to eat any fruit at all. The prohibition, based on hygienic reasons, always appeared to me to have been issued because John Pontifex was particularly fond of fruit.

"I 'mourn not, Johnnie," he said, taking a bite out of the right-hand apple; "I mourn not for her who is departed. Rather," he added, with emphasis, biting into the left-hand apple, "I rejoice—ahem—with exceeding great joy." Whether he rejoiced because she was gone, or because of an assurance of her future, did not appear on the face of his statement. What he added was more obscure still. "Next year," he said, with a noise which might have been a sob and might have been a chuckle, "Next year I shall have all those—ahem —those apples and strawberries to myself, Johnnie."

Shortly after this conversation he entertained at dinner the Rev. Mr. Broughton, the Captain, and myself. It is noteworthy that the "beverage" of which his wife would never allow him to partake was on this occasion, and many subsequent occasions, freely produced. In fact, I should say, from recollection only, that he and his brother clergyman despatched a bottle and a half each. It was orthodox Port, but indubitably inferior to that possessed by the Perpetual Curate of St. Faith's.

One thing pleased Mr. Pontifex mightily to relate at that dinner. An unfortunate curate, enthusiastic, but young, had the Sunday before preached a discourse in which his rev. senior fancied he saw glimpses of Tractarianism. So he waited till the misguided youth came out of the vestry, and then said to him, before the church-wardens and a small gathering of friends :

"Well, that was—ahem—a most infamous sermon of yours."

And then he walked away, leaving the poor young man to seek such explanations and apologies as he pleased.

"The Tractarians," he said to-night, after the first bottle had brought up the natural pallor of his cheek to a ghastly whiteness, "the Tractarians may use their arguments as they please, but to me they fall off as water from the back of the—ahem —the proverbial duck, though I have never yet, I confess, poured anything but gravy upon the back of that—ahem—toothsome delicacy, and therefore am not in a position to assert that water actually does run off their backs."

"The Tractarians," said the Perpetual Curate, whose face was quite purple, "are the Actarians. They are up and doing. They will make a clear sweep of pastors like me and idle shepherds like you, Brother Pontifex."

And now they are both gone, and the Perpetual Curate's prophecy has come true, and the Church has been reformed, with, of course, a small gathering of the foolish who want to go on beyond the bounds of reason. Such a service as I knew at St. Faith's would be impossible now even in the sleepiest City church. The duet between the Parson and the Clerk has ceased, the choir is trained, the hymns are improved, and the people are attentive. Speaking as a musician, I do not find the change altogether for the best. I miss the old melancholy hymns of Wesleyan origin which we used to sing. It seems to me that life is sad, the note of rapture at which we strike so many of the new hymns is strained and unreal. We are still too much like the poor little charity children of my youth, when, after the three long services of the day, through which they had been cuffed and caned into attention, they had to sing as a concluding or parting hymn—

> " Oh ! may our earthly Sabbaths prove
> A foretaste of our joys above."

I find, but then I am only a humble organist in a country town, and never go about in the world, but for myself I find too much elation, too much joy, to suit the grey tints and sombre colours of the working and sorrowing world.

Mr. Pontifex, the type of the old high-and-dry Calvinist, whose life was as strait-laced as his doctrine, with whom laughter was a sin, and every innocent recreation an occasion for repentance, is gone, and his place knows him no more.

Mr. Broughton, the jolly old parson of the high-and-dry Church type, who enjoyed all that can be enjoyed by a scholar and a Christian in the world, strong in his firm and undoubting belief that the doctrines of the Church, faithfully held, avail unto justification, has gone too. We have none like him now. I am not a theologian, and, in Church matters, doubtless a fool. Nevertheless, I venture to say that I regret and mourn his loss. He was not only a gentleman—there are plenty of gentlemen still in the Church—he was not only a man of pure life and benevolent conduct, but he was a scholar. And I look in vain for scholars—*rari nantes in gurgite vasto*—in these later days. Here one, there one; but—ah! the old Greek scholar, massive and critical, is no longer to be found even among the sleeves of lawn; such scholars as we have mostly run to history—a study which Mr. Broughton held to be vain and illusory, except

when it was the History of the Chosen People—
and as regards all but modern history, fruitless,
because history, he thought, repeats itself, and
everything new has all been done before.

"We have Hume," he used to say; "we have
Gibbon; we have Robertson; and we have the
grand histories in Greek and Latin of the days
when men were great. What more can one want?
Let us sit down and read them; let us teach the
boys to read them; and let us leave to restless
witlings the task of labouring in a worn-out field."

Restless witlings! Dear me! Suppose Mr.
Broughton had lived to the present day!

Others have passed away who twenty years ago
took part in the drama that I have tried, with pen
unpractised, to relate. The two brothers Brambler
sleep side by side in the new cemetery, cut off in
their vigour, Ferdinand from a cold caught while
in the excess of his zeal noting the incidents of a
review during a hailstorm; Augustus from a sort
of grief consumption which seized him at the death
of his brother. He "never joyed after;" and
though on Sunday afternoons he still maintained

the imaginary state and splendour of a "gentleman sitting over his wine" at the front window, it was a performance which brought him no pleasure but that of mournful reminiscence. And so he drooped and died, trusting that he would be remembered by posterity for his services in the Legal.

Friends there were who took charge of the little ones, from Forty-four to Fifty-three. And they all did well. My especial friend, Forty-four, is married, and has a row of children like herself, as apple-faced, as cheery, and as sanguine. I hope they will do better than their grandfather. She is good enough to maintain her old friendship towards myself, undiminished by the love she bears her husband and her offspring, and confides to me all her joys and sorrows.

Let me pass to the last scene of my story.

After Celia married, and the regiment went away, the good old Captain began to droop. He was nearly seventy years of age, it is true, but I thought he was hale and hearty—good for ten years more.

That was not so. Age crept upon him with stealth, but with swiftness. He still went out every morning, but his afternoon walks were gradually shortened, and finally had to be dropped altogether.

Then his friends began to call in the evening to talk to, and cheer up, the old man. Mr. Broughton would come with a story and anecdote of bygone days; one or two old naval men, chums of his youth, would drop in for a glass of grog and a yarn; we became hospitable, and kept open house. And all went well, in spite of increasing weakness, until one day it became apparent that the old man could not go out to make his morning round.

Then, for the first time, I learned from him, though I had long known it, what the morning round had been, for more than twenty years.

He sat feebly in his arm-chair, patient, under the inevitable. Nothing was wrong with him, but the weakness of extreme old age. His mind was bright and clear, as the last runnings of a cask of some noble vintage; but on this morning he realised that he must not think of going out any more, as he had been wont, in fair weather and foul. A cold east wind blew down the street, and a bright sun shone without warmth from a steel-blue sky.

"The end is growing near, Laddy," he said. "They will miss me when I am gone."

"Who, sir?" I asked.

He was silent for a space, thinking.

"To all of us," he said, "the Lord giveth His gifts in trust. To me He gave, besides Her Majesty's pension of two hundred pounds a year, a private fortune. No need to talk about it to you, Laddy, or to Leonard. It was not a great fortune, only this house and a hundred pounds a year, which my father saved up out of his pay. It was in the old prize days."

I began to understand.

"So long as you and Leonard were boys," the Captain went on, "we had the pension to live upon. Plenty for us all. And there was the hundred a year for which I was a trustee, you know. When you began to make an income the pension became part of the Trust——"

"Of course, sir, I quite see that."

"That made three hundred a year. A good deal ought to be done with such a sum. I doubt whether I have done the best—but I have tried—I have tried. If a man tries to do his Duty—he may be stupid—but if he tries, the Chief knows. You will find out, when I am gone, how far I have done the best, Laddy. It will be yours, the hundred a year and the house; you will use it, my boy, as you think best—not to follow up my lines, unless you think that the best way, but as a Trust from the Lord, unless your income fails, when it will keep you from want. No, Laddy, no need to promise. We have not lived together for five-and-twenty years for me to begin distrusting. But, if you can, look after them, my boy. They are ignorant, they have no friends; they are degraded; you will meet at first with all sorts of insult and disappointment; but go on, never leave them; and you will end, as I have done, by winning their confidence."

I did not ask him who "they" were, partly because I guessed. The old seaport town had dens of wickedness in it of which I have said nothing. Indeed, as children, though we went daily through the streets which reeked with every abominable thing, we saw and knew nothing—how should we? It is the blessed prerogative of innocence that it plays unhurt in the den of wild beasts, rides upon the lion, and walks scatheless among the rabble rout of Comus.

All that morning the Captain sat in disquiet. The current of his daily thoughts was interrupted. After our mid-day dinner, he refused his pipe of tobacco and sat in the window, gazing silently upon the Milldam pool, crisped by the cold east wind. His work was over; nothing more for him to do but to sit in the chair and wait for the end. That must be a solemn moment in a man's life, when he realises that everything is finished. The record complete, the book of work shut up, and after all attempted and achieved, the inevitable feeling of unprofitable service.

Two days passed; the east wind continued, and grew colder; there was no hint at any possibility of going out; and on the third day there came, creeping stealthily, a deputation consisting of two women, to ask after the Captain. They stood shame-faced at the door, and when I asked them to enter and see him, they hesitated and looked at each other. Then they came in, looking strange and abashed. I took them to the Captain, where he sat in his arm-chair, and left them with him.

Presently, sitting in the other room, I heard sobs and cries.

Afterwards others came, not always outcasts: old greybeards who had been sailors, some of the wooden-legged veterans whom I remembered as a boy, aged women, their wives and widows, even young fellows, sailors themselves, their sons and grandsons. Among them all one woman who came oftenest and stayed the longest. I remembered her as the black-haired fury who, as Leonard had reminded me, came one evening, and made the night air horrible with imprecations. Now she was subdued, now she sat as long as we would let her, silent and gazing with her black and deep-set eyes in the old man's face. It matters nothing about her history, which may be guessed—there is a dreadful similarity about these stories : an emotional, impulsive woman who loved and hated, sinned and repented, with the same ardour and vehemence, who believed in the Captain, whose patience she had sorely tried, as one believes a Gospel. He was her Gospel.

The end came more quickly than we expected. One morning I saw a change, and telegraphed for

Leonard and Celia to come quickly. The Captain knew, I think, that his last day had dawned, for he asked me when we had dressed him if I would send for "the boy" and Celia.

They could not arrive before the afternoon. We allowed no one to see him except the one who would not be denied, and she sat crouched in a corner of the room, her arms round her knees, looking at the feeble figure in the arm-chair.

The Captain spoke little, he suffered no pain, he was perfectly cheerful.

"Do you think they will come in time, Laddy?" he asked. "I should like to see them before I go."

Presently he slept, and so passed away the morning unconsciously, the black eyes of the woman watching him from the corner. Outside there were gathered knots of twos and threes, the women, the old salts, the outcasts, waiting sadly for news.

Leonard and Celia came at last. The old man woke as he heard "the boy's" voice, and eagerly held out his hand.

"Don't cry, my pretty. Don't cry, Celia, my dear," he whispered. "To every man his turn, and then we separate for a while—a little while, Celia and then we shall all be together,—you and Leonard and Laddy and I—all together, dear. Never to part again."

He was growing weaker every moment. I gave him a little wine. As Celia knelt at his feet, and laid her head upon his right hand, the other woman, as if jealous, crept stealthily from her corner and seized the left. The Captain looked down on both, turned from one to the other, and then, disengaging his hands, laid one on either head, as if with a solemn blessing, equal alike for Martha or for Magdalene.

"Laddy," he murmured, "put on my uniform coat and cap, and give me my sword."

It was his fancy that he would die in the uniform of which he was so proud. We dressed him in the coat with epaulettes ; we pinned on his medals, we laid his sword across his knees, and we placed his undress cap upon his head. And then we stood round him in tearful silence.

Presently a shiver ran through his limbs.

" Leonard "—his voice was very low now—"take the sword. It is all I leave you. God bless you, Leonard—Laddy—Celia—and you——" His hand felt out as if for the poor woman who threw herself forward with sobs and passionate crying.

And then a strange thing happened. His voice, which had been sinking to a faint murmur, suddenly grew full again, and strong. He lifted his figure, and sat upright. His eyes flashed with a sudden light as he raised his voice and looked upwards. He lifted his right hand to the peak of his cap—the old familiar salute of a sailor—as he reported himself.

"Come aboard, sir!"

Then his hand dropped, and his head fell forward. The Captain was dead.

*   *   *   *   *   *   *

We buried him in the old parish churchyard, a mile from the town. Leonard's mother lay there, somewhere among the paupers ; Wassielewski slept there in peace, Poland at làst forgotten ; Wassielewski's victim lay there too. The brand-new cemetery, which they opened a year or so later, would have been no fitting place for the remains of one who in death as well as in life should be among his fellow-men. And in that great heap of bones, coffins, and human dust, piled five feet above the level of the road, we laid the Captain. It was not without a certain fitness that his grave lay next to the Paupers' Acre. When the great Resurrection shall take place the Captain shall lift his head with the ignoble and unknown herd for whom he gave his substance, and march along with them to that merciful Judge who knows the secret of every heart.

While we were yet half a mile from the church the funeral procession was stopped. There was a crowd of old sailors and people of every degree, but chiefly of the lowest; some of them stopped the hearse, and others, opening the doors of the carriages, invited the occupants to descend. We complied, wondering. They quickly formed themselves into procession. First went the old tars, two and two, stumping on wooden legs, then came a band, then the coffin borne on the shoulders of sailors, sons of those who marched first; on the pall were the Captain's cocked hat and his sword, and then we, the mourners, fell in.

The big drum, muffled, gives the signal—boum— boum! How many times before had that March from *Saul* awakened my soul to the glory and mystery of death ; the knell of warning, the wail of sorrow, the upward cry of yearning faith—and now I can never hear it without my thoughts flying back to the old man before whose honoured remains a grateful and lamenting folk did this reverence.

Boum—boum—boum.   A man who loved his fellow-men is dead.   He will bring no more words of counsel, no more exhortations to duty—no more comfort for the afflicted, no more solace for the outcast.   Boum—boum—boum.   Wail and weep, clarions, with us whose hearts are sore.   Boum—boum—boum.   And yet it is but for a season.   Change, oh music inspired of God, the souls of those who mourn till they become the souls of those who trust.

We are at the lych-gate.   Mr. Broughton—none other—waits to read the service.

" I am the Resurrection and the Life——"

From every lane and court, from every ship in harbour, from every street, the mourners are gathered together : in the presence of Death, in the graveyard, in the hopes of immortality, we are all equal; all brothers and sisters. The women weep aloud, there is not one who is unrepentant now; the tears run down the faces of the grizzled men who are standing by the grave of their brave and single-hearted old officer; none in all the world to harbour an evil thought, to raise an accusing word, against the man of seventy summers who lies in yon black coffin. Throw flowers upon him; pile the lid with flowers, with every flower a tear. The flowers will be crushed and killed by the cold clay, but the memory of the Captain shall be green.

And of all the mourners around that grave there were none—there could be none—who mourned the Captain more deeply, who loved him better, who owed him more—than the two boys whom he had picked from the very gutter, to bring them up in the fear of God and the sense of duty.

When Mr. Broughton came to certain words in the service his voice fell, and his speech was choked for a moment. Then he cleared his throat, and looking round upon the folk, read out in clear and triumphant tones, as if the words should at once bring admonition, as well as joy and consolation and hope for all of us :

"*In sure and certain hope of the Resurrection to Eternal Life.*"

THE END.

Printed by Joseph Billing and Sons.

OPINIONS OF THE LONDON PRESS

ON THE

NOVELS WRITTEN BY THE AUTHORS OF

"BY CELIA'S ARBOUR."

OPINIONS OF THE PRESS

ON

"THE GOLDEN BUTTERFLY."

"The humour of the American miner seems to have taken the place in fiction formerly occupied by Irish wit or Scotch quiet craftiness, just as the Yankee with his cool courage and ready pistol has supplanted the Englishman on the foreign stage. The authors of 'The Golden Butterfly' have brought him to London, and made him the central character of a book full of quaint conceits, startling extravagances and contrasts, and delightful humour. Our readers must seek for themselves the end of it all. 'The Golden Butterfly' will certainly add to the happiness of mankind, for we defy anybody to read it with a gloomy countenance."—*The Times*.

"'The Golden Butterfly' is one of the liveliest novels we have lately had the pleasure of reading. Of course it is professedly an extravaganza rather than a picture of real life, yet there is a great deal of real life contained in it. The characters are at once effective and original; and, although frequently they savour of caricature, there is little or nothing in their drawing that is false to nature. Such chapters as those where Mr. Beck recalls his journalistic experiences in the Far West, or dashes off with a flowing tongue an episode in the biography of his swindling countrymen whom he has stumbled upon in a London club, may be pronounced in their way almost inimitable. But there is no touch of dulness in the volumes from beginning to end, so that when we close them we feel personally grateful to the authors."—*Saturday Review*.

"That this is an exceedingly clever novel we imagine that no one who has read it, either as it appeared in weekly instalments in this journal, or in its collected and reprinted shape, is likely to deny. There is more humour and more point in it than in a score of the average fictions of the circulating library."—*The World*.

"The authors have accomplished the feat of so limning their eccentric Yankee that we get to like him cordially, and to see him as a ruined man marry a refined English lady without even a sceptical shrug of the shoulders. As long as they can draw Phillises and Gilead P. Becks, they will not want readers, or an adequate popularity at the circulating libraries, with the pecuniary reward thereto appertaining."—*The Spectator*.

"The result is not a smug modern photograph in which every-day features and costumes are reproduced with a more than Chinese servility of imitation, but a painting full of originality, with strong lights and bold shading, the colours not always well chosen or faultlessly laid on, the drawing not unfrequently incorrect, and yet the whole picture showing unmistakable signs of talent, if not of genius. Good romance writers are not too common among us."—*The Standard*.

"The flutterings of 'The Golden Butterfly' in its progress through the *World* are probably familiar already to a good many people, and we suppose that the book may be called a clever book without much danger of protest from anybody. We don't think that any one will regret having read the book."—*The Academy*.

"The twins are perhaps the best drawn of the odd people into whose company 'The Golden Butterfly' allures us, though the lines of the satire are drawn so broadly as to verge on caricature. Indeed, the reader is tempted at times to take the whole story as a burlesque. As a burlesque it is bright, clever, and amusing."—*Pall Mall Gazette*.

"The shrewd and amusing writers of 'Ready-money Mortiboy' have broken new ground in 'The Golden Butterfly.' They carry their readers to California, where their hero strikes oil by the help of his luck and a golden butterfly, given him by an Indian quaw."—*Daily News*.

"The Golden Butterfly' is clever and vivacious, with many amusing scenes, notably Mr. Beck's great dinner, at which Jack introduces a number of his friends—Mr. Carlyle, Mr. Tennyson, Mr. Swinburne, Mr. Ruskin, Mr. Sala, Mr. Darwin, Professor Huxley, and Mr. Leighton."—*Examiner*.

Published by CHATTO AND WINDUS, PICCADILLY, W.

Cloth extra. 6s. : Boards. 2s.

"The best novel is that wherein the normal conditions of human life are wrought into natural but interesting circumstances, not one where you have to be assured beforehand that such and such things did really happen, and that the work is so far faithful—that is, photographic rather than creative, and odd rather than natural. Of Jack Armstrong, this poor little 'Son of Vulcan,' whose birth cost his mother her life, and whose father was lying a heap of smouldering ashes, having set fire to his house while drunk, just at the moment when he was born, we can only say that he is a very comely picture of the ideal young man, strong and tender, manly and honest. His conduct with Mrs. Merrion, however, writes him down a companion of Dogberry on this side; but he makes amends for his folly by his goodness; and, after all, even the best young men are mostly fools in the hands of clever and unscrupulous women, handsome and their seniors. Myles Cuolahan, too, is good, but a more composite, and therefore less harmonious character than Jack. In spite of its inequalities, much of the work in 'This Son of Vulcan' is very good."—*Saturday Review.*

"The love of the young people, interrupted with due difficulties, the discovery of the villainy of Bayliss, and recovery by the rightful heir of his property, follow in due course. Everything turns out well. The authors are kind-hearted, and do not punish even their greatest villains with that severity which the law of fiction, according to certain critics, demands, but deal with them in a more amiable spirit and with a large liberality. Jack and Norah are rewarded for their virtues by all the pleasant things which life can bestow—fortune, love, happiness. There is force and vigour in these sketches. The scenes represented, though melodramatic and glaring, are dashed off with happy impetuosity. The authors have a graphic power of description, and sufficient artistic skill to group well their incidents and characters—for the most part studied from nature, evidently."—*Pall Mall Gazette.*

"There is plenty of matter in this story, of incident and of character. It can hardly be said that there is a plot, if this means any complication which even pretends to baffle or surprise the reader. But there is a story, and it is sufficiently interesting. The characters are vigorously drawn. Paul Bayliss and Myles Cuolahan are both well drawn. So is 'Cardiff Jack.' The story of his ending is a curious psychological and physiological study, which looks like reality."—*Spectator.*

"Not a little of the popularity which the authors of 'Ready-money Mortiboy' have obtained as novelists may be attributed to the reality of the actors in the stirring scenes conjured up by them. In their story of 'This Son of Vulcan' there is not a single character who might not have been drawn from life. 'This Son of Vulcan' is unquestionably a well-told tale."—*Illustrated London News.*

"'This Son of Vulcan' is a work that will be read and will outlive a season. As we have said, the story is admirably constructed. The characters are not puppets, but true presentments of mankind. Some of the scenes display great dramatic power. It is, perhaps, rather ungenerous to be critical, for we have read 'This Son of Vulcan' with pleasure, and we recommend it as a clever and fascinating novel, worthy of the reputation of the authors of 'Ready-money Mortiboy.'"—*Figaro.*

"We regret that we can linger no longer over this interesting story. Its merit is exceptional. It is rich in exciting incident, without being sensational; tender and pathetic at times, without becoming sentimental; true, and sometimes almost too true, to nature, and well and graphically written. We trust that we have said enough to encourage readers to judge of it for themselves, and we think that few who can appreciate a thoroughly sound and interesting novel will quarrel with the opinion we have expressed."—*The Hour.*

"There is true tragic terror, which reminds the reader of some of the most powerful passages of Victor Hugo, in the description of Cardiff Jack tying little Armstrong to the wreck of an old barge, and sitting down on the shore opposite with a pipe in his mouth to watch the tide coming in and gradually drowning his victim. That our readers' feelings may not be too much harrowed, we may as well tell them that the miscreant fell asleep before the waters rose to the poor boy's chin, and that long before he awoke the old barge drifted out to sea, where Jack Armstrong was rescued by a fishing boat. The writers of 'This Son of Vulcan' have won, and justly won, a high position in the world of letters."—*Standard.*

Published by CHATTO AND WINDUS, PICCADILLY, W.

Cloth extra, 6s.; Boards, 2s.

"WITH HARP AND CROWN."

"As for the tale, it is a succession of brilliant tableaux : perhaps the authors might say in answer to this objection that they were right because it is the panorama of a life. Let all the excellences of the book be noted first : Great power of description—that is to say, a faculty for word-painting such as brings the scene before the reader's eye, and this shall be presently proved. Intense sense of humour—and, oh! if the passage were not a page or two in length that assertion should be proved also. Pathos—like Dickens when Dickens forgot to try to be pathetic. 'With Harp and Crown' is a pure, wholesome, charming story, with sufficient interest to make it exciting, and containing wonderfully lifelike and vivid pictures of modern society amongst the middle classes. Nobody who once begins it will lay it down until the end has been reached."—*Morning Post.*

"A new novel by the clever authors of 'Ready-money Mortiboy' is a genuine treat for the subscribers to the circulating libraries, and I can promise some very pleasant hours to those who order 'With Harp and Crown.' As in the previous works, there is much genuine humour and pathos ; indeed, few writers that I know are capable of producing such good comic writing. Order the book by all means, without loss of time. It is most amusing."—*Judy.*

"Though there is nothing in 'With Harp and Crown' quite so good in our opinion as certain scenes and chapters here and there in 'My Little Girl,' it is a more even and complete work as a whole, it hangs better together, and the interest is perhaps better sustained. Marion Revel is a heroine who would outweigh many imperfections in a novel, nor in her case have we to regret that a fine conception has been marred by weak or clumsy execution. Her story is a very sad one ; yet sad as Marion's story is, the general tone and character of the book is anything but sad ; for Fred Revel, the brother, with his meandering search after some gentlemanly occupation befitting the head of an ancient French family—a search which generally conducts him into some West-End billiard-room—Dicky Carew, the literary hack, and, last not least, Dr. Joseph Chacomb, the man whose career so sweetly exemplifies the uses, not of adversity, but of prosperity, are all more or less comic in their way, and are drawn with a great deal of humour. The novel is one that we have read with much pleasure, and that we can recommend with confidence to our readers' attention."—*The Graphic.*

"The authors have contrived to combine merits popularly supposed to be incompatible. Their style has mellowed since the production of their deservedly successful 'Ready-money Mortiboy.' The humour is richer and more subdued, and tempered with a judicious, pleasing admixture of delicate, wholesome sentiment. To say that they have placed themselves indisputably at the head of living humourists—in the solid sense of the term—would be but poor praise ; we can, however, go much further, and maintain that our authors supply with dignity the gap in current literature hitherto left by the loss of Thackeray and Dickens. 'With Harp and Crown' merits more than the most brilliant ephemeral success—namely, a permanent and honourable place in the classical literature of the country. We find therein liveliness of manner united with seriousness of purpose, keen discernment of the rottenness of society evinced without either coarseness or cynicism; and a remarkable reserve of power."—*Examiner.*

"It is a phenomenon really worth notice that we should have in England two authors who work so wonderfully well together as the 'eminent hands' which have given us 'Ready-money Mortiboy,' 'My Little Girl,' and which now give us 'With Harp and Crown.' The freshness of imagination, the epigrammatic felicity, the novelty of thought, and the grateful absence of anything hackneyed or conventional in the narrative, are as conspicuous in 'With Harp and Crown' as in 'My Little Girl,' which, on the whole, we preferred to 'Ready-money Mortiboy.' Like Fred Revel, who wins immortal fame in the Franco-Prussian war, Sir Joseph Chacomb, and indeed all the *dramatis personæ*, improve with prosperity. 'My friends,' we are told, 'it is only in copybooks that people get punished in the material manner.' 'With Harp and Crown' is thus for the romantically sympathetic reader an eminently comfortable novel. *But it is far more than this. Rich in observation, full of knowledge of the world, abounding in consummately clever sketches of character, it is a novel which, while it will entertain every one, will also leave every one the better for having read it. From first to last it is a conscientious as well as successful piece of literary workmanship.*"—*The Hour.*

A Catalogue of American and Foreign Books Published or Imported by MESSRS. SAMPSON LOW & CO. *can be had on application.*

Crown Buildings, 188, Fleet Street, London, November, 1877.

𝔄 𝔏𝔦𝔰𝔱 𝔬𝔣 𝔅𝔬𝔬𝔨𝔰

PUBLISHED BY

SAMPSON LOW, MARSTON, SEARLE, & RIVINGTON.

————◆————

ALPHABETICAL LIST.

A CLASSIFIED Educational Catalogue of Works published in Great Britain. Demy 8vo, cloth extra. Second Edition, revised to the year 1877, 5*s.*

Abney (Captain W. de W., R.E., F.R.S.) Thebes, and its Five Greater Temples. Forty large Permanent Photographs, with descriptive letter-press. Super-royal 4to, cloth extra, 63*s.*

Adventures of Captain Mago. A Phœnician's Explorations 1000 years B.C. By LEON CAHUN. Numerous Illustrations. Crown 8vo, cloth extra, gilt, 7*s. 6d.*

Adventures of a Young Naturalist. By LUCIEN BIART, with 117 beautiful Illustrations on Wood. Edited and adapted by PARKER GILLMORE. Post 8vo, cloth extra, gilt edges, New Edition, 7*s. 6d.*

Adventures in New Guinea. The Narrative of the Captivity of a French Sailor, Louis Trégance, among the Savages in the Interior. Small post 8vo, with Illustrations and Map, cloth, gilt, 6*s.*

Africa, and the Brussels Geographical Conference. Translated from the French of EMILE BANNING, by R. H. MAJOR, F.S.A. With Map, crown 8vo, 7*s. 6d.*

Alcott (Louisa M.) Aunt Jo's Scrap-Bag. Square 16mo, 2*s. 6d.* (Rose Library, 1*s.*)

———— *Cupid and Chow-Chow.* Small post 8vo, 3*s. 6d.*

———— *Little Men: Life at Plumfield with Jo's Boys.* By the Author of "Little Women." Small post 8vo, cloth, gilt edges, 2*s. 6d.* (Rose Library, 1*s.*)

———— *Little Women.* 2 vols., 2*s. 6d.* each. (Rose Library, 2 vols., 1*s.* each.)

———— *Old-Fashioned Girl.* Best Edition, small post 8vo, cloth extra, gilt edges, 2*s. 6d.* (Rose Library, 2*s.*)

———— *Work and Beginning Again.* A Story of Experience. 1 vol., small post 8vo, cloth extra, 6*s.* Several Illustrations. (Rose Library, 2 vols., 1*s.* each.)

Alcott (*Louisa M.*) *Beginning Again*. A Sequel to "Work." 1s.
—— *Shawl Straps*. Small post 8vo, cloth extra, gilt, 3s. 6d.
—— *Eight Cousins; or, the Aunt Hill*. Small post 8vo, with Illustrations, 3s. 6d.
—— *The Rose in Bloom*. Small post 8vo, cloth extra, 3s. 6d.
—— *Silver Pitchers*. Small post 8vo, cloth extra, 3s. 6d.
—— *Under the Lilacs*. In monthly parts, price 6d.
    "Miss Alcott's stories are thoroughly healthy, full of racy fun and humour . . . . exceedingly entertaining . . . . We can recommend the 'Eight Cousins'"—*Athenæum*.
Andersen (*Hans Christian*) *Fairy Tales*. With Illustrations in Colours by E. V. B. Royal 4to, cloth, 25s.
Andrews (*Dr.*) *Latin-English Lexicon*. 14th Edition. Royal 8vo, pp. 1670, cloth extra, price 18s.
Anecdotes of the Queen and Royal Family. Collected and Edited by J. G. HODGINS, with Illustrations. New Edition, 5s.
Animals Painted by Themselves. Adapted from the French of Balzac, Louis Baude, G. Droz, Jules Janin, &c., with 200 Illustrations by GRANDVILLE. 8vo, cloth extra, gilt, 10s. 6d.
Art of Reading Aloud (*The*) *in Pulpit, Lecture Room, or Private* Reunions, with a perfect system of Economy of Lung Power on just principles for acquiring ease in Delivery, and a thorough command of the Voice. By G. VANDENHOFF, M.A. Crown 8vo, cloth.
Atmosphere (*The*). *See* FLAMMARION.

THE BAYARD SERIES.

Comprising Pleasure Books of Literature produced in the Choicest Style as Companionable Volumes at Home and Abroad.
    "We can hardly imagine better books for boys to read or for men to ponder over."—*Times*.
    Price 2s. 6d. each Volume, complete in itself, flexible cloth extra, gilt edges, with silk Headbands and Registers.
The Story of the Chevalier Bayard. By M. DE BERVILLE.
De Joinville's St. Louis, King of France.
The Essays of Abraham Cowley, including all his Prose Works.
Abdallah; or the Four Leaves. By EDOUARD LABOULLAYE.
Table-Talk and Opinions of Napoleon Buonaparte.
Vathek: An Oriental Romance. By WILLIAM BECKFORD.
The King and the Commons. A Selection of Cavalier and Puritan Songs. Edited by Prof. MORLEY.
Words of Wellington: Maxims and Opinions of the Great Duke.
Dr. Johnson's Rasselas, Prince of Abyssinia. With Notes.
Hazlitt's Round Table. With Biographical Introduction.
The Religio Medici, Hydriotaphia, and the Letter to a Friend.
    By Sir THOMAS BROWNE, Knt.

The Bayard Series, continued :—

Ballad Poetry of the Affections. By ROBERT BUCHANAN.

Coleridge's Christabel, and other Imaginative Poems. With Preface by ALGERNON C. SWINBURNE.

Lord Chesterfield's Letters, Sentences, and Maxims. With Introduction by the Editor, and Essay on Chesterfield by M. DE STE.-BEUVE, of the French Academy.

Essays in Mosaic. By THOS. BALLANTYNE.

My Uncle Toby; his Story and his Friends. Edited by P. FITZGERALD.

Reflections ; or, Moral Sentences and Maxims of the Duke de la Rochefoucauld.

*Socrates, Memoirs for English Readers from Xenophon's Memo-*rabilia. By EDW. LEVIEN.

Prince Albert's Golden Precepts.

　　A suitable Case containing 12 *Volumes, price* 31s. 6d *; or the Case separately, price* 3s. 6d.

BEAUTY and the Beast. An Old Tale, with Pictures by E. V. B. Demy 4to, cloth extra, novel binding. 10 Illustrations in Colours. 12s. 6d.

Beumer's German Copybooks. In six gradations at 4d. each.

Bickersteth's Hymnal Companion to Book of Common Prayer. A new Edition, with 160 Additional Hymns and numerous new tunes, has been issued; the Original Editions are kept in print. An 8pp. prospectus and price lists will be sent post free on application.
　　*** A liberal allowance is made to Clergymen.

Bickersteth (Rev. E. H., M.A.) The Reef and other Parables. 1 vol., square 8vo, with numerous very beautiful Engravings, uniform in character with the Illustrated Edition of Heber's Hymns, &c., 7s. 6d.

———— *The Master's Home-Call; or, Brief Memorials of* Alice Frances Bickersteth. 20th Thousand. 32mo, cloth gilt, 1s.

———— *The Shadow of the Rock.* A Selection of Religious Poetry. 18mo, cloth extra, 2s. 6d.

———— *The Clergyman in his Home.* Small post 8vo, 1s.

———— *The Shadowed Home and the Light Beyond.* 6th Edition, crown 8vo, cloth extra, 5s.

Bida. The Authorized Version of the Four Gospels, with the whole of the magnificent Etchings on Steel, after drawings by M. BIDA, in 4 vols., appropriately bound in cloth extra, price 3l. 3s. each. Also the four volumes in two, bound in the best morocco, by Suttaby, extra gilt edges, 18l. 18s., half-morocco, 12l. 12s.

Bidwell (C. T.) The Balearic Islands. Illustrations and a Map. Crown 8vo, cloth, 10s. 6d.

———— *The Cost of Living Abroad.* Crown 8vo, 6s.

Black (Wm.) Three Feathers. Small post 8vo, cloth extra, 6s.

Black (*Wm.*) *Lady Silverdale's Sweetheart, and other Stories.* 1 vol., crown 8vo, 10s. 6d.

———— *Kilmeny: a Novel.* Small post 8vo, cloth, 6s.

———— *In Silk Attire.* 3rd Edition, small post 8vo, 6s.

———— *A Daughter of Heth.* 11th Edition, crown 8vo, cloth extra, 6s. With Frontispiece by F. WALKER, A.R.A.

Blackmore (*R. D.*) *Lorna Doone.* 10th Edition, cr. 8vo, 6s.

———— *Alice Lorraine.* 1 vol., small post 8vo, 6th Edition, 6s.

———— *Clara Vaughan.* Revised Edition, 6s.

———— *Cradock Nowell.* New Edition, 6s.

———— *Cripps the Carrier.* 3rd Edition, small post 8vo, 6s.

———— *Georgics of Virgil.* Small 4to, 4s. 6d.

Blue Banner (*The*); *or, The Adventures of a Mussulman, a* Christian, and a Pagan, in the time of the Crusades and Mongol Conquest. By LEON CAHUN. Translated from the French by W. COLLETT SANDARS. With Seventy-six Wood Engravings. 1 vol., square imperial 16mo, cloth extra, 7s. 6d.

Book of the Play. By DUTTON COOK. 2 vols., crown 8vo, 24s.

Brett (*E.*) *Notes on Yachts.* Fcp., 6s.

Bryant (*W. C., assisted by S. H. Gay*) *A Popular History of* the United States. About 4 vols., to be profusely Illustrated with Engravings on Steel and Wood, after Designs by the best Artists. Vol. I., super-royal 8vo, cloth extra, gilt, 42s., is ready.

Burnaby (*Capt. Fred*). *See* On Horseback through Asia.

Burton (*Captain R. F.*) *Two Trips to Gorilla Land and the* Cataracts of the Congo. By Captain R. F. BURTON. 2 vols, demy 8vo, with numerous Illustrations and Map, cloth extra, 28s.

Butler (*W. F.*) *The Great Lone Land; an Account of the Red* River Expedition, 1869-70. With Illustrations and Map. Crown 8vo, cloth extra, 7s. 6d.

———— *The Wild North Land; the Story of a Winter Journey* with Dogs across Northern North America. Demy 8vo, cloth, with numerous Woodcuts and a Map, 4th Edition, 18s. Crown 8vo, 7s. 6d.

———— *Akim-foo: the History of a Failure.* Demy 8vo, cloth, 2nd Edition, 16s. Also, in crown 8vo, 7s. 6d.

By Land and Ocean; or, The Journal and Letters of a Tour round the World by a Young Girl. By F. L. RAINS. Crown 8vo, cloth, 7s. 6d.

*C*ADOGAN (*Lady A.*) *Illustrated Games of Patience.* Twenty-four Diagrams in Colours, with Descriptive Text. Foolscap 4to, cloth extra, gilt edges, 3rd Edition, 12s. 6d.

Cahun (*Leon*) *Adventures of Captain Mago.* *See* Adventures.

Cahun (Leon) Blue Banner, which see.

Ceramic Art. See JACQUEMART.

Changed Cross (The), and other Religious Poems. 2*s.* 6*d.*

Child's Play, with 16 Coloured Drawings by E. V. B. Printed on thick paper, with tints, 7*s.* 6*d.*

———— *New*, which see.

Choice Editions of Choice Books. 2*s.* 6*d.* each, Illustrated by C. W. COPE, R.A., T. CRESWICK, R.A., E. DUNCAN, BIRKET FOSTER, J. C. HORSLEY, A.R.A., G. HICKS, R. REDGRAVE, R.A., C. STONEHOUSE, F. TAYLER, G. THOMAS, H. J. TOWNSHEND, E. H. WEHNERT, HARRISON WEIR, &c.

Bloomfield's Farmer's Boy. | Milton's L'Allegro.
Campbell's Pleasures of Hope. | Poetry of Nature. Harrison Weir.
Coleridge's Ancient Mariner. | Rogers' (Sam.) Pleasures of Memory.
Goldsmith's Deserted Village. | Shakespeare's Songs and Sonnets.
Goldsmith's Vicar of Wakefield. | Tennyson's May Queen.
Gray's Elegy in a Churchyard. | Elizabethan Poets.
Keat's Eve of St. Agnes. | Wordsworth's Pastoral Poems.

"Such works are a glorious beatification for a poet."—*Athenæum.*

Clara Vaughan. Revised Edition, 6*s. See* BLACKMORE.

Collins (Mortimer): His Letters and Friendships, with some Account of his Life. By FRANCES COLLINS. 2 vols., crown 8vo, with a Portrait, 2nd Edition, 21*s.*

"The impression conveyed is pleasant as well as favourable."—*Athenæum.*
"These charming volumes."—*Standard.*
"It is a very fascinating and attractive work."—*John Bull.*

Cook (D.) Young Mr. Nightingale. A Novel. 3 vols., 31*s.* 6*d.*

———— *The Banns of Marriage.* 2 vols., crown 8vo, 21*s.*

———— *Book of the Play.* 2 vols., crown 8vo, 24*s.*

———— *Doubleday's Children.* 3 vols., crown 8vo, 31*s.* 6*d.*

Cradock Nowell. New Edition, 6*s. See* BLACKMORE.

Cripps the Carrier. 3rd Edition, 6*s. See* BLACKMORE.

Cruise of H.M.S. "Challenger" (The). By W. J. J. SPRY, R.N. With Route Map and many Illustrations. 4th Edition. In 1 vol., demy 8vo, cloth extra, price 18*s.*

Cumming (Miss C. F. G.) From the Hebrides to the Himalayas; Eighteen Months' Wanderings in Western Isles and Eastern Highlands. By Miss CONSTANCE F. GORDON CUMMING, with very numerous Full-page and other Woodcut Illustrations, from the Author's own Drawings. 2 vols., medium 8vo, cloth extra, 42*s.*

Cyclopædia of Education (The); A Dictionary of Information for the use of Teachers, School Officers, Parents, and others. Edited by HENRY KIDDLE and ALEXANDER J. SCHEM. Complete in 1 vol., demy 8vo, cloth extra, 21*s.*

DANA (R. H.) Two Years before the Mast and Twenty-four years After. Revised Edition with Notes. 12mo. 6*s.*

Dana (Jas. D.) Corals and Coral Islands. Numerous Illustrations, Charts, &c. New and Cheaper Edition, with numerous important Additions and Corrections. Crown 8vo, cloth extra, 8s. 6d.

Daughter (A) of Heth. By WILLIAM BLACK. 13th and Cheaper Edition. 1 vol., crown 8vo, 6s.

Day of my Life (A); or, Every Day Experiences at Eton. By an ETON BOY. Super-royal 16mo, cloth, 2s. 6d. 6th Thousand.

Discoveries of Prince Henry the Navigator, and their Results; being the Narrative of the Discovery by Sea, within One Century, of more than Half the World. By RICHARD HENRY MAJOR, F.S.A. Demy 8vo, with several Woodcuts, 4 Maps, and a Portrait of Prince Henry in Colours. Cloth extra, 15s.

"Mr. R. H. Major has supplied a serious gap in our biographical literature. . . . . One of the most interesting volumes of biography we have yet had under review."—*Daily Telegraph.*

Dodge (Mrs. M.) Hans Brinker; or, the Silver Skates. An entirely New Edition, with 59 Full-page and other Woodcuts. Square crown 8vo, cloth extra, 7s. 6d.; Text only, paper, 1s.

—— *Theophilus and Others.* 1 vol., small post 8vo, cloth extra, gilt, 3s. 6d.

ENGLISH Catalogue of Books (The). Published during 1863 to 1871 inclusive, comprising also the Important American Publications.

This Volume, occupying over 450 Pages, shows the Titles of 32,000 New Books and New Editions issued during Nine Years, with the Size, Price, and Publisher's Name, the Lists of Learned Societies, Printing Clubs, and other Literary Associations, and the Books issued by them; as also the Publisher's Series and Collections—altogether forming an indispensable adjunct to the Bookseller's Establishment, as well as to every Learned and Literary Club and Association. 30s., half-bound.

*** The previous Volume, 1835 to 1862, of which very few remain on sale, price 2l. 5s.; as also the Index Volume, 1837 to 1857, price 1l. 6s.

—— *Supplements,* 1863, 1864, 1865, 3s. 6d. each; 1866, 1867 to 1876, 5s. each.

Eight Cousins. See ALCOTT.

English Painters of the Georgian Era. Hogarth to Turner. Biographical Notices. Illustrated with 48 permanent Photographs, after the most celebrated Works. Demy 4to, cloth extra, 18s.

FAITH Gartney's Girlhood. By the Author of "The Gayworthys." Fcap. with Coloured Frontispiece, 3s. 6d.

Familiar Letters on some Mysteries of Nature. See PHIPSON.

Fern World (The). By FRANCIS GEORGE HEATH, Author of "The Fern Paradise," "The English Peasantry," &c. Illustrated by Twelve Coloured Plates, giving complete Figures (Sixty-four in all) several full-page Engravings of some of the choicest Scenery in Devon ; and a permanent Photographic Frontispiece. Large post 8vo., handsomely bound in cloth, gilt edges, 400 pages, 2nd Edition, 12s. 6d.

Few (A) Hints on Proving Wills. Enlarged Edition, 1s.

Fish and Fishing. By J. J. MANLEY, M.A. Crown 8vo, with Illustrations, 10s. 6d.

Five Weeks in Greece. By J. F. YOUNG. Crown 8vo, 10s. 6d.

Flammarion (C.) The Atmosphere. Translated from the French of CAMILLE FLAMMARION. Edited by JAMES GLAISHER, F.R.S., Superintendent of the Magnetical and Meteorological Department of the Royal Observatory at Greenwich. With 10 Chromo-Lithographs and 81 Woodcuts. Royal 8vo, cloth extra, 30s.

Footsteps of the Master. See STOWE (Mrs. BEECHER).

Forrest (John) Explorations in Australia. Being Mr. JOHN FORREST's Personal Account of his Journeys. 1 vol., demy 8vo, cloth, with several Illustrations from the Author's Sketches, drawn on wood by G. F. ANGAS, and 3 Maps, 16s.

Forrest's (R. W.) Gleanings from the Pastures of Tekoa. By the Rev. R. W. FORREST, D.D., Vicar of St. Jude's, South Kensington. 1 vol., small post 8vo, 260 pp., cloth extra, 6s.

Franc (Maude Jeane) Emily's Choice : an Australian Tale. 1 vol., small post 8vo. With a Frontispiece by G. F. ANGAS, 5s.

———— *Hall's Vineyard.* Small post 8vo, cloth, 4s.

———— *John's Wife: a Story of Life in South Australia.* Small post 8vo, cloth extra, 4s.

———— *Marian; or, the Light of Some One's Home.* Fcap. 8vo, 3rd Edition, with Frontispiece, 5s.

———— *Silken Cords and Iron Fetters.* 4s.

———— *Vermont Vale.* Small post 8vo., with Frontispiece, 5s.

———— *Minnie's Mission.* Small post 8vo, with Frontispiece, 4s.

———— *Little Mercy.* Small post 8vo, 5s.

GAMES of Patience. See CADOGAN.

Garvagh (Lord) The Pilgrim of Scandinavia. By LORD GARVAGH, B.A. 8vo, cloth extra, with Illustrations, 10s. 6d.

Gayworthys (The) : a Story of New England Life. Small post 8vo, 3s. 6d.

Gentle Life (Queen Edition). 2 vols. in 1, small 4to, 10s. 6d.

THE GENTLE LIFE SERIES.

Printed in Elzevir, on Toned Paper, handsomely bound, forming suitable Volumes for Presents. Price 6s. each ; or in calf extra, price 10s. 6d.

The Gentle Life. Essays in aid of the Formation of Character of Gentlemen and Gentlewomen. 21st Edition.

The Gentle Life Series, continued :—

About in the World.   Essays by Author of "Gentle Life."

Like unto Christ.   A New Translation of Thomas à Kempis'
"De Imitatione Christi."   With a Vignette from an Original Drawing
by Sir THOMAS LAWRENCE.   2nd Edition.

Familiar Words.   An Index Verborum, or Quotation Handbook.   Affording an immediate Reference to Phrases and Sentences
that have become embedded in the English language.   3rd and
enlarged Edition.
   "The most extensive dictionary of quotation we have met with."—*Notes and
Queries.*

Essays by Montaigne.   Edited, Compared, Revised, and
Annotated by the Author of "The Gentle Life."   With Vignette Portrait.   2nd Edition.
   "We should be glad if any words of ours could help to bespeak a large circula-
tion for this handsome attractive book."—*Illustrated Times.*

The Countess of Pembroke's Arcadia.   Written by Sir PHILIP
SIDNEY.   Edited by the Author of "The Gentle Life."   7s. 6d.

The Gentle Life.   2nd Series, 8th Edition.

Varia : Readings from Rare Books.
   "The books discussed in this volume are no less valuable than they are rare, and
the compiler is entitled to the gratitude of the public."—*Observer.*

The Silent Hour : Essays, Original and Selected.   By the
Author of "The Gentle Life."   3rd Edition.

Half-Length Portraits.   Short Studies of Notable Persons.
By GIBSON CRAIG.   Small post 8vo, cloth extra, 6s.

Essays on English Writers, for the Self-improvement of
Students in English Literature.
   "To all (both men and women) who have neglected to read and study their native
literature we would certainly suggest the volume before us as a fitting introduction.'
—*Examiner.*

Other People's Windows.   By J. HAIN FRISWELL.   3rd Edition.
   "The chapters are so lively in themselves, so mingled with shrewd views of
human nature, so full of illustrative anecdotes, that the reader cannot fail to be
amused."—*Morning Post.*

A Man's Thoughts.   By J. HAIN FRISWELL.

German Primer.   Being an Introduction to First Steps in
German.   By M. T. PREU.   2s. 6d.

Getting On in the World ; or, Hints on Success in Life.   By
WILLIAM MATHEWS, LL.D.   Small post 8vo, cloth extra, 2s. 6d.;
gilt edges, 3s. 6d.

Gleams through the Mists ; Literary and Domestic.   By C.
BICKERSTETH WHEELER, Author of "John Lang Bickersteth,"
"Taking the Consequences," &c.   Post 8vo, cloth extra, 3s. 6d.

Gouffé. The Royal Cookery Book. By JULES GOUFFÉ; translated and adapted for English use by ALPHONSE GOUFFÉ, Head Pastrycook to Her Majesty the Queen. Illustrated with large plates printed in colours. 161 Woodcuts, 8vo, cloth extra, gilt edges, 2l. 2s.

————— Domestic Edition, half-bound, 10s. 6d.

"By far the ablest and most complete work on cookery that has ever been submitted to the gastronomical world."—*Pall Mall Gazette.*

————— *The Book of Preserves; or, Receipts for Preparing and Preserving* Meat, Fish salt and smoked, Terrines, Gelatines, Vegetables, Fruit, Confitures, Syrups, Liqueurs de Famille, Petits Fours, Bonbons, &c., &c. 1 vol., royal 8vo, containing upwards of 500 Receipts and 34 Illustrations, 10s. 6d.

————— *Royal Book of Pastry and Confectionery.* By JULES GOUFFÉ, Chef-de-Cuisine of the Paris Jockey Club. Royal 8vo, Illustrated with 10 Chromo-lithographs and 137 Woodcuts, from Drawings by E. MONJAT. Cloth extra, gilt edges, 35s.

Gouraud (Mdlle.) Four Gold Pieces. Numerous Illustrations. Small post 8vo, cloth, 2s. 6d. *See also* Rose Library.

Gower (Lord Ronald) Handbook to the Art Galleries, Public and Private, of Belgium and Holland. 18mo, cloth, 5s.

————— *The Castle Howard Portraits.* 2 vols., folio, cl. extra, 6l. 6s.

Greek Grammar. See WALLER.

Guizot's History of France. Translated by ROBERT BLACK. Super-royal 8vo, very numerous Full-page and other Illustrations. In 5 vols., cloth extra, gilt, each 24s.

"It supplies a want which has long been felt, and ought to be in the hands of all students of history."—*Times.*

"Three-fourths of M. Guizot's great work are now completed, and the 'History of France,' which was so nobly planned, has been hitherto no less admirably executed."—*From long Review of Vol. III. in the Times.*

————— *History of England.* In 3 vols. of about 500 pp. each, with 60 to 70 Full-page and other Illustrations, cloth, gilt, 24s. each.

"For luxury of typography, plainness of print, and beauty of illustration, these volumes, of which but one has as yet appeared in English, will hold their own against any production of an age so luxurious as our own in everything, typography not excepted."—*Times.*

Guillemin. See World of Comets.

Guyon (Mad.) Life. By UPHAM. 6th Edition, crown 8vo, 6s.

————— *A Short Method of Prayer and Spiritual Torrents.* Translated from the French original of Madame DE LA MOTHE GUYON. 12mo, cloth extra, 2s.

HACKLANDER (F. W.) Bombardier H. and Corporal Dose; or, Military Life in Prussia. Translated from the German of F. W. HACKLANDER. Crown 8vo, cloth extra, 5s.

Handbook to the Charities of London. See LOW's.

————— *Principal Schools of England. See* Practical.

Half-Length Portraits. Short Studies of Notable Persons. By GIBSON CRAIG. Small post 8vo, cloth extra, 6s.

Hall (S. P.) Sketches from an Artist's Portfolio. See Sketches.

Hall (W. W.) How to Live Long; or, 1408 *Health Maxims,* Physical, Mental, and Moral. By W. W. HALL, A.M., M.D. Small post 8vo, cloth, 2s. Second Edition.

"We can cordially commend it to all who wish to possess the *mens sana in corpore sano."—Standard.*

Hans Brinker; or, the Silver Skates. See DODGE.

Hazlitt (William) The Round Table. Bayard Series, 2s. 6d.

Heber's (Bishop) Illustrated Edition of Hymns. With upwards of 100 beautiful Engravings. Small 4to, handsomely bound, 7s. 6d. Morocco, 18s. 6d. and 21s.

Hector Servadac. See VERNE. The heroes of this story were carried away through space on the Comet "Gallia," and their adventures are recorded with all Jules Verne's characteristic spirit.

☞ This copyright work will not be produced in any cheaper form than this for some time to come.

Henderson (A.) Latin Proverbs and Quotations; with Translations and Parallel Passages, and a copious English Index. By ALFRED HENDERSON. Fcap. 4to, 530 pp., 10s. 6d.

History and Handbook of Photography. Translated from the French of GASTON TISSANDIER. Edited by J. THOMSON. Imperial 16mo, over 300 pages, 70 Woodcuts, and Specimens of Prints by the best Permanent Processes, cloth extra, 6s. Second Edition, with an Appendix by the late Mr. HENRY FOX TALBOT, giving an account of his researches.

History of a Crime (The); Deposition of an Eye-witness. By VICTOR HUGO. 2 vols., crown 8vo. This work, which is in fact a history of the "The Coup d'Etat," was written at Brussels in December, 1851, January and February, 1852. M. Hugo was president of the Council of Resistance. He has here stated all that he did with his friends and everything he saw, day by day and hour by hour. The work is as dramatic as a romance, and as startling as the reality it relates, and that reality has the interest and grandeur of one of the most considerable events of the nineteenth century, which has had such an enormous influence over France and the whole of Europe.

—— *England.* See GUIZOT.

—— *France.* See GUIZOT.

—— *Merchant Shipping.* See LINDSAY.

—— *United States.* See BRYANT.

Hitherto. By the Author of " The Gayworthys." New Edition, cloth extra, 3s. 6d. Also, in Rose Library, 2 vols., 2s.

Hofmann (Carl) A Practical Treatise on the Manufacture of Paper in all its Branches. Illustrated by 110 Wood Engravings, and 5 large Folding Plates. 4to, cloth, 400 pages, 3l. 13s. 6d.

How to Live Long. See HALL.

Hugo (Victor). See History of a Crime.

Hugo (Victor) "Ninety-Three." Translated by FRANK LEE BENEDICT and J. HAIN FRISWELL. New Edition. Illustrated. One vol, crown 8vo, 6s.

—— *Toilers of the Sea.* Crown 8vo. Illustrated, 6s. ; fancy boards, 2s. ; cloth, 2s. 6d. ; On large paper with all the original Illustrations, 10s. 6d.

Hymnal Companion to Book of Common Prayer. See BICKERSTETH.

ILLUSTRATIONS of China and its People. By J. THOMSON, F.R.G.S. Being 200 permanent Photographs from the Author's Negatives, with Letterpress Descriptions of the Places and People represented. Four Volumes imperial 4to, each 3l. 3s.

Is that All ? By a well-known American Author. Small post 8vo, cloth extra, 3s. 6d.

JACQUEMART (A.) History of the Ceramic Art : Descriptive and Analytical Study of the Potteries of all Times and of all Nations. By ALBERT JACQUEMART. 200 Woodcuts by H. Catenacci and J. Jacquemart. 12 Steel-plate Engravings, and 1000 Marks and Monograms. Translated by Mrs. BURY PALLISER. In 1 vol., super-royal 8vo, of about 700 pp., cloth extra, gilt edges, 28s.

"This is one of those few gift-books which, while they can certainly lie on a table and look beautiful, can also be read through with real pleasure and profit."—*Times.*

KENNEDY'S (Capt. W. R.) Sporting Adventures in the Pacific. With Illustrations, demy 8vo, 18s.

Khedive's Egypt (The) ; or, The old House of Bondage under New Masters. By EDWIN DE LEON, Ex-Agent and Consul-General in Egypt. In 1 vol., demy 8vo, cloth extra, Second Edition, 18s.

Kingston (W. H. G.). See Snow-Shoes.

—— *Child of the Cavern.*

—— *Two Supercargoes.*

Koldewey (Capt.) The Second North German Polar Expedition in the Year 1869-70. Numerous Woodcuts, Maps, and Chromolithographs. Royal 8vo, cloth extra, 1l. 15s.

LADY Silverdale's Sweetheart. See BLACK.

Land of Bolivar (The) ; or, War, Peace, and Adventure in the Republic of Venezuela. By JAMES MUDIE SPENCE, F.R.G.S., F.Z.S. 2 vols., demy 8vo, cloth extra, with numerous Woodcuts and Maps, 31s. 6d.

Landseer Gallery (The). Containing thirty-six Autotype Reproductions of Engravings from the most important early works of Sir EDWIN LANDSEER. With a Memoir of the Artist's Life, and Descriptions of the Plates. Imperial 4to, handsomely bound in cloth, gilt edges, 2l. 2s.

Leared (A.) Morocco and the Moors. Being an Account of Travels, with a Description of the Country and its People. By ARTHUR LEARED, M.D. With Illustrations, 8vo, cloth extra, 18s.

Le-Duc (V.) How to build a House. By VIOLLET-LE-DUC, Author of "The Dictionary of Architecture," &c. Numerous Illustrations, Plans, &c. 1 vol., medium 8vo, cloth, gilt edges, 2nd Edition, 12s.

———— *Annals of a Fortress.* Numerous Illustrations and Diagrams. Demy 8vo, cloth extra, 15s.

———— *The Habitations of Man in all Ages.* By E. VIOLLET-LE-DUC. Illustrated by 103 Woodcuts. Translated by BENJAMIN BUCKNALL, Architect. 8vo, cloth extra, 16s.

———— *Lectures on Architecture.* By VIOLLET-LE-DUC. Translated from the French by BENJAMIN BUCKNALL, Architect. In 2 vols., royal 8vo, 3l. 3s. Also in Parts, 10s. 6d. each.

———— *Mont Blanc: a Treatise on its Geodesical and Geological Constitution*—its Transformations, and the Old and Modern state of its Glaciers. By EUGENE VIOLLET-LE-DUC. With 120 Illustrations. Translated by B. BUCKNALL. 1 vol., demy 8vo, 14s.

———— *On Restoration.* By VIOLLET-LE-DUC, with a Notice of his Works in connexion with the Historical Monuments of France. By CHARLES WETHERED. Crown 8vo, with a Portrait on Steel of VIOLLET-LE-DUC, cloth extra, 2s. 6d.

Life and Letters of the Honourable Charles Sumner (The). 2 vols., royal 8vo, cloth. The Letters give full description of London Society—Lawyers—Judges—Visits to Lords Fitzwilliam, Leicester, Wharncliffe, Brougham—Association with Sydney Smith, Hallam, Macaulay, Dean Milman, Rogers, and Talfourd.—The work also contains a full Journal which Sumner kept in Paris. 36s.

Lindsay (W. S.) History of Merchant Shipping and Ancient Commerce. Over 150 Illustrations, Maps and Charts. In 4 vols., demy 8vo, cloth extra. Vols. 1 and 2, 21s. each; vols. 3 and 4, 24s. each; 4 vols., 4l. 10s.

"Another standard work."—*Times.*

Lion Jack: a Story of Perilous Adventures amongst Wild Men and Beasts. Showing how Menageries are made. By P. T. BARNUM. With Illustrations. Crown 8vo, cloth extra, price 6s.

Little King; or, the Taming of a Young Russian Count. By S. BLANDY. Translated from the French. 64 Illustrations. Crown 8vo, cloth extra, gilt, 7s. 6d.

"There is a great deal worth reading in this book."—*Pall Mall Gazette.*
"A very pleasant and interesting volume, which we would recommend to our readers."—*Spectator.*

Little Mercy; or, For Better for Worse. By MAUDE JEANNE FRANC, Author of "Marian," "Vermont Vale," &c., &c. Small post 8vo, cloth extra.

Long (Col. C. Chaillé) Central Africa. Naked Truths of Naked People: an Account of Expeditions to Lake Victoria Nyanza and the Mabraka Niam-Niam. Demy 8vo, numerous Illustrations, 18s.

Low's German Series.

The attention of the Heads of Colleges and Schools is directed to this New Series of German School Books, which has been projected with a view to supply a long-felt want, viz., thoroughly reliable Text-Books, edited by German scholars of the highest reputation, at a price which will bring them within the reach of all. The Series comprises:—

1. **The Illustrated German Primer.** Being the easiest introduction to the study of German for all beginners. *1s.*
2. **The Children's own German Book.** A Selection of Amusing and Instructive Stories in Prose. Edited by Dr. A. L. MEISSNER, Professor of Modern Languages in the Queen's University in Ireland. Small post 8vo, cloth, *1s. 6d.*
3. **The First German Reader, for Children from Ten to Fourteen.** Edited by Dr. A. L. MEISSNER. Small post 8vo, cloth, *1s. 6d.*
4. **The Second German Reader.** Edited by Dr. A. L. MEISSNER, Small post 8vo, cloth, *1s. 6d.*

Buchheim's Deutsche Prosa. Two Volumes, sold separately:—

5. **Schiller's Prosa.** Containing Selections from the Prose Works of Schiller, with Notes for English Students. By Dr. BUCHHEIM, Professor of the German Language and Literature, King's College, London. Small post 8vo, *2s. 6d.*
6. **Goethe's Prosa.** Containing Selections from the Prose Works of Goethe, with Notes for English Students. By Dr. BUCHHEIM. Small post 8vo, *3s. 6d.*

Low's Standard Library of Travel and Adventure. Crown 8vo, bound uniformly in cloth extra, price *7s. 6d.*

1. **The Great Lone Land.** By W. F. BUTLER, C.B.
2. **The Wild North Land.** By W. F. BUTLER, C.B.
3. **How I found Livingstone.** By H. M. STANLEY.
4. **The Threshold of the Unknown Region.** By C. R. MARKHAM. (4th Edition, with Additional Chapters, *10s. 6d.*)
5. **A Whaling Cruise to Baffin's Bay and the Gulf of Boothia.** By A. H. MARKHAM.
6. **Campaigning on the Oxus.** By J. A. MACGAHAN.
7. **Akim-foo: the History of a Failure.** By MAJOR W. F. BUTLER, C.B.
8. **Ocean to Ocean.** By the Rev. GEORGE M. GRANT. With Illustrations.

Low's Standard Novels. Crown 8vo, *6s.* each, cloth extra.

Three Feathers. By WILLIAM BLACK.
A Daughter of Heth. 13th Edition. By W. BLACK. With Frontispiece by F. WALKER, A.R.A.
Kilmeny. A Novel. By W. BLACK.
In Silk Attire. By W. BLACK.
Alice Lorraine. By R. D. BLACKMORE.
Lorna Doone. By R. D. BLACKMORE. 8th Edition.
Cradock Nowell. By R. D. BLACKMORE.
Clara Vaughan. By R. D. BLACKMORE.

Low's Standard Novels, continued :—

Cripps the Carrier. By R. D. BLACKMORE.

Innocent. By Mrs. OLIPHANT. Eight Illustrations.

Work. A Story of Experience. By LOUISA M. ALCOTT. Illustrations. *See also* Rose Library.

Mistress Judith. A Cambridgeshire Story. By C. C. FRAZER-TYTLER.

Never Again. By Dr. MAYO, Author of "Kaloolah."

Ninety-Three. By VICTOR HUGO. Numerous Illustrations.

My Wife and I. By Mrs. BEECHER STOWE.

Low's Handbook to the Charities of London for 1877. Edited and revised to July, 1877, by C. MACKESON, F.S.S., Editor of "A Guide to the Churches of London and its Suburbs," &c. 1*s.*

MACGAHAN (J. A.) Campaigning on the Oxus, and the Fall of Khiva. With Map and numerous Illustrations, 4th Edition, small post 8vo, cloth extra, 7*s.* 6*d.*

———— *Under the Northern Lights ; or, the Cruise of the* "Pandora." With Illustrations. Demy 8vo, cloth extra, 18*s.*

Macgregor (John) "Rob Roy" on the Baltic. 3rd Edition, small post 8vo, 2*s.* 6*d.*

———— *A Thousand Miles in the "Rob Roy" Canoe.* 11th Edition, small post 8vo, 2*s.* 6*d.*

———— *Description of the "Rob Roy" Canoe,* with Plans, &c., 1*s.*

———— *The Voyage Alone in the Yawl "Rob Roy."* 2nd Edition, small post 8vo, 5*s.*

Markham (A. H.) A Whaling Cruise to Baffin's Bay and the Gulf of Boothia. With an Account of the Rescue of the Crew of the "Polaris." 3rd Edition, crown 8vo, 2 Maps and Illustrations, cloth, 7*s.* 6*d.*

Markham (C. R.) The Threshold of the Unknown Region. Crown 8vo, with Four Maps, 4th Edition, with Additional Chapters. Cloth extra, 10*s.* 6*d.*

Maury (Commander) Physical Geography of the Sea, and its Meteorology. Being a Reconstruction and Enlargement of his former Work, with Charts and Diagrams. New Edition, crown 8vo, 6*s.*

Men of Mark : a Gallery of Permanent Photographic Portraits of the most Eminent Men of the Day taken from Life. In Monthly Parts, price 1*s.* 6*d.*

———— Vols. I. and II. for 1876 and 1877, containing 36 Portraits each. 4to, cloth extra, gilt, 25*s.*

Mercy Philbrick's Choice. Small post 8vo, 3*s.* 6*d.*

"The story is of a high character, and the play of feeling is very subtilely and cleverly wrought out."—*British Quarterly Review.*

Michael Strogoff.   10s. 6d.   *See* VERNE.

Mistress Judith.   A Cambridgeshire Story.   By C. C. FRASER-
TYTLER, Author of "Jasmine Leigh "   A New and Cheaper Edition
in 1 vol., small post 8vo, cloth extra, 6s.

Mohr (E.) To the Victoria Falls of the Zambesi.   By EDWARD
MOHR.   Translated by N. D'ANVÉRS.   Numerous Woodcut Illustrations, four beautiful Chromo-lithographs and a Map.   8vo, cloth, 24s.

Mongolia, Travels in.   *See* PREJAVALSKY.

Montaigne's Essays.   *See* Gentle Life Series.

My Brother Jack; or, The Story of Whatd'yecallem.   Written
by Himself.   From the French of ALPHONSE DAUDET.   Illustrated
by P. PHILIPPOTEAUX.   Square imperial 16mo, cloth extra, 7s. 6d.

> " He would answer to Hi ! or to any loud cry,
> To What-you-may-call-'em, or What was his name ;
> But especially Thingamy-jig."—*Hunting of the Snark.*

My Rambles in the New World.   By LUCIEN BIART, Author of
"The Adventures of a Young Naturalist."   Translated by MARY DE
HAUTEVILLE.   Crown 8vo, cloth extra.   Numerous Full-page Illustra-
tions, 7s. 6d.

*N*APOLEON I., *Recollections of.*   By Mrs. ABELL.   3rd
Edition.   Demy 8vo, with Steel Portrait and Woodcuts, cloth
gilt, 10s. 6d.

Napoleon III. in Exile.   Posthumous Works and Unpub-
lished Autographs.   Collected and arranged by COUNT DE LA
CHAPELLE.   8vo, cloth extra, 14s.

New Ireland.   By A. M. SULLIVAN, M.P. for Louth.   2 vols.,
demy 8vo, cloth extra, 30s.   One of the main objects which the
Author has had in view in writing this work has been to lay before
England and the world a true and faithful history of Ireland, or rather
a series of descriptive sketches of the numerous eventful episodes in
Ireland's career during the last quarter of a century.

New Testament.   The Authorized English Version ; with
various readings from the most celebrated Manuscripts, in English.
With Notes by the Editor, Dr. TISCHENDORF.   Cloth flexible, gilt
edges, 2s. 6d. ; cheaper style, 2s. ; or sewed, 1s. 6d.

Noble Words and Noble Deeds.   Translated from the French of
E. MULLER, by DORA LEIGH.   Containing many Full-page Illustrations by PHILIPPOTEAUX.   Square imperial 16mo, cloth extra, 7s. 6d.

> " This is a book which will delight the young. . . . We cannot imagine a nicer
> present than this book for children."—*Standard.*
> " Is certain to become a favourite with young people."—*Court Journal.*

Notes and Sketches of an Architect taken during a Journey in the
North-West of Europe.   Translated from the French of FELIX NAR-
JOUX. 214 Full-page and other Illustrations. Demy 8vo, cloth extra, 16s.

> " His book is vivacious and sometimes brilliant. It is admirably printed and

Notes on Fish and Fishing. By the Rev. J. J. MANLEY, M.A.
With Illustrations, crown 8vo, cloth extra, leatherette binding, 10s. 6d.
"We commend the work."—*Field.*
"He has a page for every day in the year, or nearly so, and there is not a dull
one amongst them."—*Notes and Queries.*
"A pleasant and attractive volume."—*Graphic.*
"Brightly and pleasantly written."—*John Bull.*

OCEAN to Ocean: Sandford Fleming's Expedition through
Canada in 1872. By the Rev. GEORGE M. GRANT. With Illustrations. Revised and enlarged, Cheaper Edition, crown 8vo, cloth, 7s. 6d.

Old-Fashioned Girl. See ALCOTT.

Old Masters. Da Vinci, Bartolomeo, Michael Angelo,
Romagna, Carlo Dolci, &c., &c. Reproduced in Photography from
Engravings in the British Museum, with Biographical Notices, by
STEPHEN THOMPSON. Imperial folio, cloth extra, 3l. 13s. 6d.

Oleographs. Catalogue and price lists post free on application.

Oliphant (Mrs.) Innocent. A Tale of Modern Life. By Mrs.
OLIPHANT, Author of "The Chronicles of Carlingford," &c., &c.
With Eight Full-page Illustrations, small post 8vo, cloth extra, 6s.

On Horseback through Asia Minor. By Capt. FRED BURNABY,
Royal Horse Guards, Author of "A Ride to Khiva." 2 vols., demy
8vo, with three Maps and Portrait of Author, cloth extra, 38s. This
work describes a ride of over 2000 miles through the heart of Asia
Minor, and gives an account of five months with Turks, Circassians,
Christians, and Devil-worshippers. 6th Edition.

Our Little Ones in Heaven. Edited by the Rev. H. ROBBINS.
With Frontispiece after Sir JOSHUA REYNOLDS. Fcap., cloth extra,
New Edition—the 3rd, with Illustrations, 5s.

Out of School at Eton. Being a collection of Poetry and Prose
Writings. By SOME PRESENT ETONIANS. Fcp. 8vo, cloth, 3s. 6d.

PAINTERS of All Schools. By LOUIS VIARDOT, and other
Writers. 500 pp., super-royal 8vo, 20 Full-page and 70 smaller
Engravings, cloth extra, 25s. A New Edition is now being issued
in Half-crown parts, with fifty additional portraits.
"A handsome volume, full of information and sound criticism."—*Times.*
"Almost an encyclopædia of painting. . . . . It may be recommended as a handy
and elegant guide to beginners in the study of the history of art."—*Saturday Review.*

Palliser (Mrs.) A History of Lace, from the Earliest Period.
A New and Revised Edition, with additional cuts and text, upwards
of 100 Illustrations and coloured Designs. 1 vol. 8vo, 3rd Edition, 1l. 1s.
"One of the most readable books of the season ; permanently valuable, always interesting, often amusing, and not inferior in all the essentials of a gift book."—*Times.*

———— *Historic Devices, Badges, and War Cries.* 8vo, 1l. 1s.

———— *The China Collector's Pocket Companion.* With upwards
of 1000 Illustrations of Marks and Monograms. 2nd Edition, with
Additions. Small post 8vo, limp cloth, 5s.
"We scarcely need add that a more trustworthy and convenient handbook does
not exist, and that others besides ourselves will feel grateful to Mrs. Palliser for the
care and skill she has bestowed upon it."—*Academy.*

Petites Leçons de Conversation et de Grammaire: Oral and Conversational Method ; being Little Lessons introducing the most Useful Topics of Daily Conversation, the French Verbs (Regular and Irregular) upon an entirely new principle, Anecdotes and Correspondence, &c. By F. JULIEN, French Master at King Edward the Sixth's Grammar School, Birmingham. Crown 8vo, cloth, 3*s.* 6*d.*

Phelps (Miss) Gates Ajar. 32mo, 6*d.*

———— *Men, Women, and Ghosts.* 12mo, sewed, 1*s.* 6*d.* ; cl., 2*s.*

———— *Hedged In.* 12mo, sewed, 1*s.* 6*d.* ; cloth, 2*s.*

———— *Silent Partner.* 5*s.*

———— *Trotty's Wedding Tour.* Small post 8vo, 3*s.* 6*d.*

———— *What to Wear.* Fcap. 8vo, fancy boards, 1*s.*

Phillips (L.) Dictionary of Biographical Reference. 8vo, 1*l.* 11*s.* 6*d.*

Phipson (Dr. T. L.) Familiar Letters on some Mysteries of Nature and Discoveries in Science. Crown 8vo, cloth extra, 7*s.* 6*d.*

Photography (History and Handbook of). See TISSANDIER.

Picture Gallery of British Art (The). 38 Beautiful and Permanent Photographs after the most celebrated English Painters. With Descriptive Letterpress. Vols. 1 to 5, cloth extra, 18*s.* each. Each separate and complete in itself.

Pike (N.) Sub-Tropical Rambles in the Land of the Aphanapteryx. In 1 vol., demy 8vo, 18*s.* Profusely Illustrated from the Author's own Sketches. Also with Maps and Meteorological Charts.

Plutarch's Lives. An Entirely New and Library Edition. Edited by A. H. CLOUGH, Esq. 5 vols.,·8vo, 2*l.* 10*s.* ; half-morocco, gilt top, 3*l.* Also in 1 vol., royal 8vo, 800 pp., cloth extra, 18*s.* ; half-bound, 21*s.*

———— *Morals.* Uniform with Clough's Edition of " Lives of Plutarch." Edited by Professor GOODWIN. 5 vols., 8vo, 3*l.* 3*s.*

Poems of the Inner Life. New Edition, with many additional Poems, inserted by permission of the Authors. Small post 8vo, cloth, 5*s.*

Polar Expeditions. See KOLDEWEY, MARKHAM, MACGAHAN.

Practical (A) Handbook to the Principal Schools of England. By C. E. PASCOE. Showing the cost of living at the Great Schools, Scholarships, &c., &c. Crown 8vo, cloth extra, 3*s.* 6*d.*
   " This is an exceedingly useful work, and one that was much wanted."— *Examiner.*

Preces Veterum. Collegit et edidit Joannes F. France. Crown 8vo, cloth, red edges, 5*s.*

Prejevalsky (N. M.) Travels in Mongolia. By N. M. PREJE-VALSKY, Lieutenant-Colonel, Russian Staff. Translated by E. DELMAR MORGAN, F.R.G.S., and Annotated by Colonel YULE, C.B. 2 vols., demy 8vo, cloth extra, numerous Illustrations and Maps, 2*l.* 2*s.*

Preu (M. T.) German Primer. Square cloth, 2*s.* 6*d.*

Price (Sir Rose, Bart.). *See* The Two Americas.

Prince Ritto ; or, The Four-leaved Shamrock. By FANNY W. CURREY. With 10 Full-page Facsimile Reproductions of Original Drawings by HELEN O'HARA. Demy 4to, cloth extra, gilt, 10s. 6d.

Publishers' Circular (The), and General Record of British and Foreign Literature. Giving a transcript of the title-page of every work published in Great Britain, and every work of interest published abroad, with lists of all the publishing-houses.

Published on the 1st and 15th of every Month, and forwarded post free to all parts of the world on payment of 8s. per annum.

Purdy (W.) The City Life, a Review of Finance and Commerce. Crown 8vo, cloth, 7s. 6d.

RALSTON (W. R. S.) Early Russian History. Four Lectures by W. R. S. RALSTON, M.A. Crown 8vo, cloth extra, 5s.

Read (S.) Leaves from a Sketch Book. Pencillings of Travel at Home and Abroad. By SAMUEL READ. Royal 4to, containing about 130 Engravings on Wood, cloth extra, 25s.

Recollections of Samuel Breck, with Passages from his Note- Books (1771—1862). Edited by H. E. SCUDDER. Cr. 8vo, cl., 10s. 6d.

Retzsch (M.) Outlines to Burger's Ballads. 15 Etchings by MORITZ RETZSCH. With Text and Notes. Oblong 4to, cloth, 10s. 6d.

—— *Outlines to Goethe's Faust.* Etchings by MORITZ RETZSCH. 26 Etchings. Oblong 4to, cloth extra, 10s. 6d.

—— *Outlines to Schiller's "Fight with the Dragon," and* "Fridolin." 26 Etchings. Oblong 4to, cloth, 10s. 6d.

—— *Outlines to Schiller's "Lay of the Bell."* 42 Etchings. With Lord Lytton's Translation. Oblong 4to, cloth, 10s. 6d.

Rose in Bloom. *See* ALCOTT.

Rose Library (The). Popular Literature of all countries. Each volume, 1s. ; cloth, 2s. 6d. Many of the Volumes are Illustrated. The following is a list :—

1. **Sea-Gull Rock.** By JULES SANDEAU. Illustrated.
2. **Little Women.** By LOUISA M. ALCOTT.
3. **Little Women Wedded.** Forming a Sequel to "Little Women."
4. **The House on Wheels.** By MADAME DE STOLZ. Illustrated.
5. **Little Men.** By LOUISA M. ALCOTT.
6. **The Old-Fashioned Girl.** By LOUISA M. ALCOTT. Double vol., 2s. ; cloth, 3s. 6d.
7. **The Mistress of the Manse.** By J. G. HOLLAND.
8. **Timothy Titcomb's Letters to Young People, Single and Married.**
9. **Undine, and the Two Captains.** By Baron DE LA MOTTE FOUQUÉ. A New Translation by F. E. BUNNETT. Illustrated.
10. **Draxy Miller's Dowry, and the Elder's Wife.** By SAXE HOLM.
11. **The Four Gold Pieces.** By Madame GOURAUD. Numerous Illustrations.

Rose Library (*The*), *continued* :—

12. **Work.** A Story of Experience. First Portion. By LOUISA M. ALCOTT.
13. **Beginning Again.** Being a Continuation of "Work." By LOUISA M. ALCOTT.
14. **Picciola; or, the Prison Flower.** By X. B. SAINTINE. Numerous Graphic Illustrations.
15. **Robert's Holidays.** Illustrated.
16. **The Two Children of St. Domingo.** Numerous Illustrations.
17. **Aunt Jo's Scrap Bag.**
18. **Stowe (Mrs. H. B.) The Pearl of Orr's Island.**
19. —— **The Minister's Wooing.**
20. —— **Betty's Bright Idea.**
21. —— **The Ghost in the Mill.**
22. —— **Captain Kidd's Money.**
23. —— **We and our Neighbours.** Double vol., 2s. Post 8vo, cloth, 3s. 6d.
24. —— **My Wife and I.** Double vol., 2s. Post 8vo, cloth, 3s. 6d.
25. **Hans Brinker; or, the Silver Skates.**
26. **Lowell's My Study Window.**
27. **Holmes (O. W.) The Guardian Angel.**
28. **Warner (C. D.) My Summer in a Garden.**
29. **Hitherto.** By the Author of "The Gayworthys." 2 vols., 1s. each.
30. **Helen's Babies.** By their Latest Victim.
31. **The Barton Experiment.** By the Author of "Helen's Babies."

Russell (*W. H., LL.D.*) *The Tour of the Prince of Wales in* India, and his Visits to the Courts of Greece, Egypt, Spain, and Portugal. By W. H. RUSSELL, LL.D. Illustrated by SYDNEY P. HALL, M.A. Super-royal 8vo, cloth extra, gilt edges, 52s. 6d.; Large Paper Edition, 84s.

SCHWEINFURTH (*Dr. G.*) *The Heart of Africa; or, Three* Years' Travels and Adventures in its Unexplored Regions. By Dr. G. SCHWEINFURTH. Translated by ELLEN E. FREWER. 2 vols., 8vo, with 130 Woodcuts from Drawings made by the Author, and 2 Maps, 2nd Edition, 42s.

—— *Artes Africanæ.* Illustrations and Descriptions of Productions of the Natural Arts of Central African Tribes. With 26 Lithographed Plates, imperial 4to, boards, 28s.

Sea-Gull Rock. By JULES SANDEAU, of the French Academy. Translated by ROBERT BLACK, M.A. With 79 very beautiful Woodcuts. Royal 16mo, cloth extra, gilt edges, 7s. 6d. Cheaper Edition, cloth gilt, 2s. 6d. *See also* Rose Library.

"It deserves to please the new nation of boys to whom it is presented."—*Times.*

Seonee : Sporting in the Satpura Range of Central India, and in the Valley of the Nerbudda. By R. A. STERNDALE, F.R.G.S. 8vo, with numerous Illustrations, 2nd Edition, 21s.

Shooting: its Appliances, Practice, and Purpose. By JAMES
DALZIEL DOUGALL, F.S.A., F.Z.A. Author of "Scottish Field
Sports," &c. Crown 8vo, cloth extra, 10s. 6d.

"The book is admirable in every way. . . . . We wish it every success."—*Globe.*
"A very complete treatise. . . . . Likely to take high rank as an authority on
shooting."—*Daily News.*

Silent Hour (The). *See* Gentle Life Series.

Silver Pitchers. *See* ALCOTT.

Six Hundred Robinson Crusoes ; or, The Voyage of the Golden
Fleece. A true Story for old and young. By GILBERT MORTIMER.
Illustrated. Post 8vo, cloth extra, 5s.

Sketches from an Artist's Portfolio. By SYDNEY P. HALL.
About 60 Facsimiles of his Sketches during Travels in various parts of
Europe. Folio, cloth extra, 3l. 3s.

"A portfolio which any one might be glad to call their own."—*Times.*

Sketches of Life and Scenery in Australia. By a Twenty-five
Years' Resident. 1 vol., crown 8vo, cloth extra, 6s.

Sleepy Sketches ; or, How we Live, and How we Do Not Live.
From Bombay. 1 vol., small post 8vo, cloth, 6s.

"Well-written and amusing sketches of Indian society."—*Morning Post.*

Smith (G.) Assyrian Explorations and Discoveries. By the late
GEORGE SMITH. Illustrated by Photographs and Woodcuts. Demy
8vo, 6th Edition, 18s.

———— *The Chaldean Account of Genesis.* Containing the
Description of the Creation, the Fall of Man, the Deluge, the Tower
of Babel, the Times of the Patriarchs, and Nimrod ; Babylonian
Fables, and Legends of the Gods ; from the Cuneiform Inscriptions.
By the late G. SMITH, British Museum. Author of "History of
Assurbanipal," "Assyrian Discoveries," &c., &c. With many Illus-
trations. Demy 8vo, cloth extra, 5th Edition, 16s.

Snow-Shoes and Canoes ; or, the Adventures of a Fur-Hunter
in the Hudson's Bay Territory. By W. H. G. KINGSTON. 2nd
Edition. With numerous Illustrations. Square crown 8vo, cloth
extra, gilt, 7s. 6d.

Spain. Illustrated by GUSTAVE DORÉ. Text by the BARON
CH. D'AVILLIER. Containing over 240 Wood Engravings by DORÉ,
half of them being Full-page size. Imperial 4to, elaborately bound
in cloth, extra gilt edges, 3l. 3s.

NOTICE.—*New Series, commenced November 1st. Price One Shilling, Monthly.*

St. Nicholas for 1878. The First Number of the New
Series of the above Magazine commenced November 1st, and on
December 1st a New Story by LOUISA M. ALCOTT, entitled "Under
the Lilacs," will be commenced. This New Series will also be
embellished with a new and very beautiful cover, designed by Mr.
WALTER CRANE.

Stanley (H. M.) How I Found Livingstone. Crown 8vo, cloth
extra, 7s. 6d. ; demy 8vo, 10s. 6d.

Stanley (H.M.) " My Kalulu," Prince, King, and Slave. A Story from Central Africa. Crown 8vo, about 430 pp., with numerous graphic Illustrations, after Original Designs by the Author. Cloth, 7s. 6d.

——— *Coomassie and Magdala.* A Story of Two British Campaigns in Africa. Demy 8vo, with Maps and Illustrations, 16s. 2nd Edition.

Sterndale (R. A.). See Seonee.

Storey's (Justice) Works. See Low's American Catalogue.

Story without an End. From the German of Carové, by the late Mrs. SARAH T. AUSTIN. Crown 4to, with 15 Exquisite Drawings by E. V. B., printed in Colours in Facsimile of the original Water Colours ; and numerous other Illustrations. New Edition, 7s. 6d.

——— square 4to, with Illustrations by HARVEY. 2s. 6d.

Stowe (Mrs. Beecher) Dred. Tauchnitz Edition. 12mo, 3s. 6d.; also in boards, 1s.

——— *Footsteps of the Master.* With Illustrations and red borders. Small post 8vo, cloth extra, 6s.

——— *Betty's Bright Idea.*

——— *My Wife and I ; or, Harry Henderson's History.* Small post 8vo, cloth extra, 6s.*

——— *Minister's Wooing,* 5s. ; Copyright Series, 1s. 6d.; cl., 2s.*

——— *Old Town Folk.* 6s. ; Cheap Edition, 2s. 6d.

——— *Old Town Fireside Stories.* Cloth extra, 3s. 6d.

——— *We and Our Neighbours.* 1 vol., small post 8vo, 6s. Sequel to "My Wife and I." *

——— *Pink and White Tyranny.* Small post 8vo, 3s. 6d. ; Cheap Edition, 1s. 6d. and 2s.

——— *Queer Little People.* 1s. ; cloth 2s.

——— *Chimney Corner.* 1s. ; cloth, 1s. 6d.

——— *The Pearl of Orr's Island.* Crown 8vo, 5s.*

——— *Little Pussey Willow.* Fcap., 2s.

——— *Woman in Sacred History.* Illustrated with 15 Chromolithographs and about 200 pages of Letterpress. Demy 4to, cloth extra, gilt edges, 25s.
    * *See also* Rose Library.

Street Life in London. By J. THOMSON, F.R.G.S., and ADOLPHE SMITH. Each Monthly Part, 4to size, in Wrapper, price 1s. 6d., contains Three Permanent Photographs, taken from Life expressly for this Periodical. Volume for 1877, 25s.
    ₊ The object of the Work is to present to the reader some account of the present condition of London Street Folk, and to supply a series of faithful pictures of the people themselves.

Sullivan (A.M., M.P.). See New Ireland.

Summer Holiday in Scandinavia (A). By E. L. L. ARNOLD. Crown 8vo, cloth extra, 10s. 6d.

Sumner (Hon. Charles). *See* Life and Letters.

TAUCHNITZ'S English Editions of German Authors. Each volume, cloth flexible, 2s. ; or sewed, 1s. 6d. Catalogues post free on application.

Textbook (A) of Harmony. For the Use of Schools and Students. By the late C. E. HORSLEY. Revised by WESTLEY RICHARDS and W. H. CALCOTT. Small post 8vo, cloth, 3s. 6d.

Thebes, and its Five Greater Temples. *See* ABNEY.

Thomson (J.) The Straits of Malacca, Indo-China, and China ; or, Ten Years' Travels, Adventures, and Residence Abroad. By J. THOMSON, F.R.G.S., Author of "Illustrations of China and its People." Upwards of 60 Woodcuts, from the Author's own Photographs and Sketches. Demy 8vo, cloth extra, 21s.

Thorne (E.) The Queen of the Colonies ; or, Queensland as I saw it. 1 vol., with Map, 6s.

Ticknor (George), Life, Letters, and Journals. 2 vols., crown 8vo, cloth extra, 21s.

"No matter what your peculiar taste in this style of composition, no matter what your range of acquirement, rest assured that you will rise from the careful perusal of his journals and correspondence with a lively sense of self-satisfaction, amused, instructed, and (we will venture to add) improved."—*Quarterly Review.*

Tissandier (Gaston) A History and Handbook of Photography. Translated from the French of GASTON TISSANDIER ; edited by J. THOMSON, F.R.G.S. Imperial 16mo, over 300 pages, and 75 Wood Engravings and a Frontispiece, cloth extra, 6s.

"This work should find a place on the shelves of every photographer's library."—*The British Journal of Photography.*
"This capital handbook will tend to raise photography once more to its true position as a science, and to a high place among the fine arts."—*The Spectator.*

Tour of the Prince of Wales in India. *See* RUSSELL.

Trollope (A.) Harry Heathcote of Gangoil. A Story of Bush Life in Australia. With Graphic Illustrations. In 1 vol., small post, cloth extra, 2nd Edition, 5s.

Turkistan. Notes of a Journey in the Russian Provinces of Central Asia and the Khanates of Bokhara and Kokand. By EUGENE SCHUYLER, Secretary to the American Legation, St. Petersburg. Numerous Illustrations. 2 vols, demy 8vo, cl. extra, 5th Edition.

Two Americas ; being an Account of Sport and Travel, with Notes on Men and Manners in North and South America. By Sir ROSE PRICE, Bart. Demy 8vo, with Illustrations, cloth extra, 2nd Edition, 18s.

"We have seldom come across book which has given us so much pleasure."—*Land and Water.*

Two Supercargoes (The) ; or, Adventures in Savage Africa. By W. H. G. KINGSTON. Square imperial 16mo, cloth extra, 7s. 6d. Numerous Full-page Illustrations.

VANDENHOFF (George, M.A.). See Art of Reading Aloud.

Verne's (Jules) Works. Translated from the French, with from 50 to 100 Illustrations. Each cloth extra, gilt edges—

Large post 8vo, price 10s. 6d. each—

1. Fur Country.
2. Twenty Thousand Leagues under the Sea.
3. From the Earth to the Moon, and a Trip round It.
4. Michael Strogoff, the Courier of the Czar.
5. Hector Servadac.

Imperial 16mo, price 7s. 6d. each—

1. Five Weeks in a Balloon.
2. Adventures of Three Englishmen and Three Russians in South Africa.
3. Around the World in Eighty Days.
4. A Floating City, and the Blockade Runners.
5. Dr. Ox's Experiment, Master Zacharius, A Drama in the Air, A Winter amid the Ice, &c.
6. The Survivors of the " Chancellor."
7. Dropped from the Clouds. ⎫
8. Abandoned. ⎬ The Mysterious Island. 3 vols., 22s. 6d.
9. Secret of the Island. ⎭
10. The Child of the Cavern.

The following Cheaper Editions are issued with a few of the Illustrations, in handsome paper wrapper, price 1s. ; cloth, gilt, 2s. each.

1. Adventures of Three Englishmen and Three Russians in South Africa.
2. Five Weeks in a Balloon.
3. A Floating City.
4. The Blockade Runners.
5. From the Earth to the Moon.
6. Around the Moon.
7. Twenty Thousand Leagues under the Sea. Vol. I.
8. ———— Vol. II. The two parts in one, cloth, gilt, 3s. 6d.
9. Around the World in Eighty Days.
10. Dr. Ox's Experiment, and Master Zacharius.
11. Martin Paz, the Indian Patriot.
12. A Winter amid the Ice.
13. The Fur Country. Vol. I.
14. ———— Vol. II. Both parts in one, cloth gilt, 3s. 6d.

The public must kindly be careful to order Low's AUTHOR'S EDITIONS.

WALLER (Rev. C. H.) The Names on the Gates of Pearl, and other Studies. By the Rev. C. H. WALLER, M.A. Crown 8vo, cloth extra, 6s.

Waller (Rev. C. H.) A Grammar and Analytical Vocabulary of the Words in the Greek Testament. Compiled from Brüder's Concordance. For the use of Divinity Students and Greek Testament Classes. By the Rev. C. H. WALLER, M.A., late Scholar of University College, Oxford. Tutor of the London College of Divinity, St. John's Hall, Highbury. Part I., The Grammar. Small post 8vo, cloth, 2s. 6d.

Warburton's (Col. Egerton) Journey across Australia. With Illustrations and a Map. Demy 8vo, cloth, 16s.

Westropp (H. M.) A Manual of Precious Stones and Antique Gems. By HODDER M. WESTROPP, Author of "The Traveller's Art Companion," "Pre-Historic Phases," &c. Numerous Illustrations. Small post 8vo, cloth extra, 6s.

Whitney (Mrs. A. D. T.) The Gayworthys. Small post 8vo, 3s. 6d.

—— *Faith Gartney.* Small post 8vo, 3s. 6d. And in Low's Cheap Series, 1s. 6d. and 2s.

—— *Real Folks.* 12mo, crown, 3s. 6d.

—— *Hitherto.* Small post 8vo, 3s. 6d. and 2s. 6d.

—— *Sights and Insights.* 3 vols., crown 8vo, 31s. 6d.

—— *Summer in Leslie Goldthwaite's Life.* Small post 8vo, 3s. 6d.

—— *The Other Girls.* Small post 8vo, cloth extra, 3s. 6d.

—— *We Girls.* Small post 8vo, 3s. 6d.; Cheap Edition, 1s. 6d. and 2s.

*Woolsey (C. D., LL.D.) Introduction to the Study of Inter-*national Law; designed as an Aid in Teaching and in Historical Studies. Crown 8vo, cloth extra, 8s. 6d.

Worcester's (Dr.) New and Greatly Enlarged Dictionary of the English Language. Adapted for Library or College Reference, comprising 40,000 Words more than Johnson's Dictionary. 4to, cloth, 1834 pp., price 31s. 6d. well bound; ditto, half-morocco, 2l. 2s.

World of Comets. By A. GUILLEMIN, Author of "The Heavens." Translated and edited by JAMES GLAISHER, F.R.S. 1 vol., super-royal 8vo, with numerous Woodcut Illustrations, and 3 Chromo-lithographs, cloth extra, 31s. 6d.

XENOPHON'S Anabasis. A Literal Translation, by G. B. WHEELER. Books I to III. Crown 8vo, boards, 2s.

—— *Books I. to VII.* Boards, 3s. 6d.

London:

SAMPSON LOW, MARSTON, SEARLE, & RIVINGTON.

CROWN BUILDINGS, 188, FLEET STREET.

Lightning Source UK Ltd.
Milton Keynes UK
UKOW01f0918071117
312328UK00007B/747/P